LOST RAILWAYS OF NORTHAMPTONSHIRE

Geoffrey Kingscott

COUNTRYSIDE BOOKS
NEWBURY, BERKSHIRE

CONTENTS

ABBREVIATIONS

The following abbreviations are used in this book:

PRE-GROUPING

E&WJR	East & West Junction Railway
GCR	Great Central Railway
GNR	Great Northern Railway
GWR	Great Western Railway
KT&HR	Kettering, Thrapston & Huntingdon Railway
L&BR	London & Birmingham Railway
LNWR	London & North Western Railway
MR	Midland Railway
N&BJR	Northampton & Banbury Junction Railway
S&MJR	Stratford-upon-Avon & Midland Junction Railway

POST-GROUPING

GWR	Great Western Railway
LMS	London, Midland & Scottish Railway
LNER	London & North Eastern Railway

POST-NATIONALISATION

BR	British Railways (later British Rail)

HERITAGE RAILWAYS

N&LR	Northampton & Lamport Railway
NVR	Nene Valley Railway

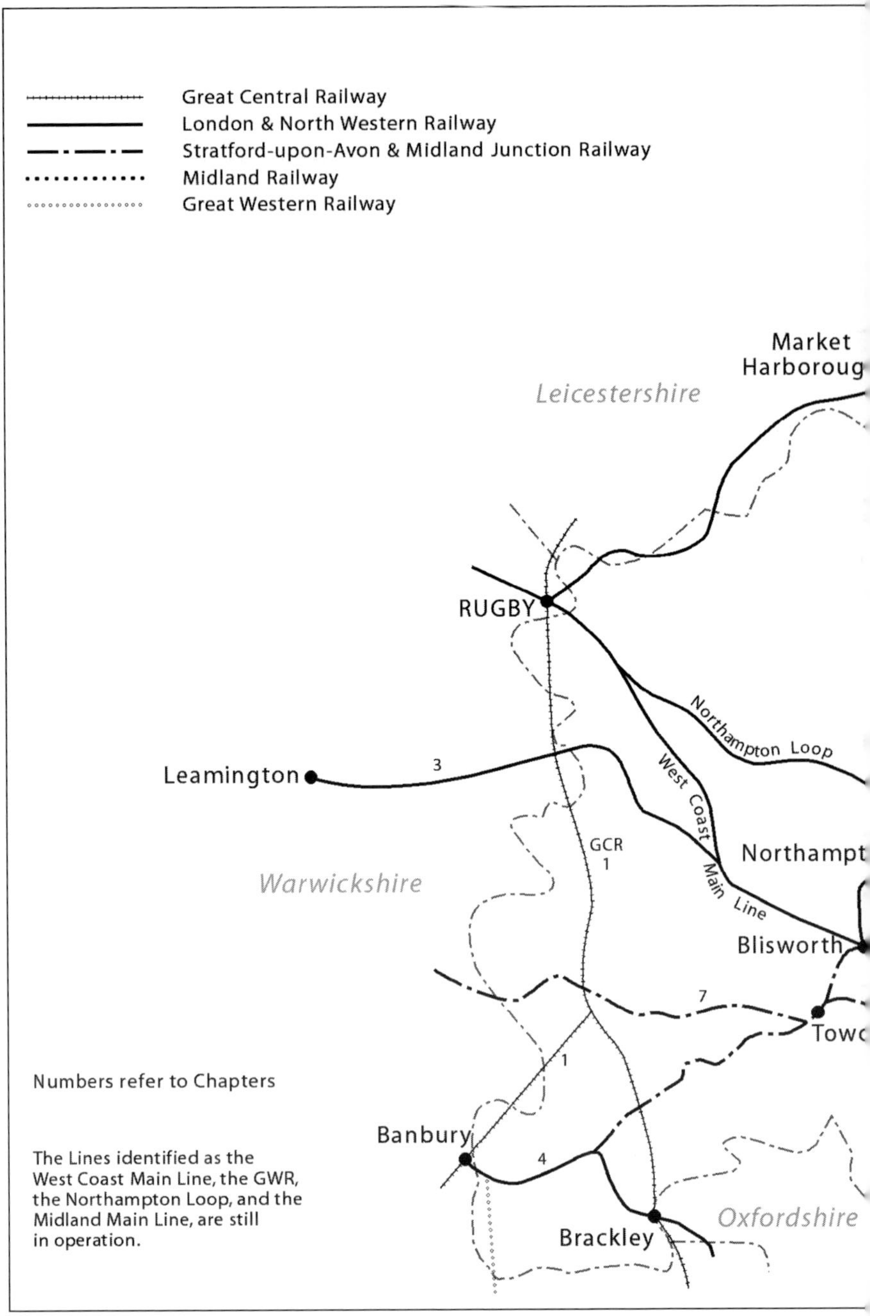

Great Central Railway
London & North Western Railway
Stratford-upon-Avon & Midland Junction Railway
Midland Railway
Great Western Railway

Market Harboroug
Leicestershire
RUGBY
Northampton Loop
West Coast Main Line
Leamington
3
GCR 1
Northampt
Warwickshire
Blisworth
7
Tow
1
Banbury
4
Brackley
Oxfordshire

Numbers refer to Chapters

The Lines identified as the
West Coast Main Line, the GWR,
the Northampton Loop, and the
Midland Main Line, are still
in operation.

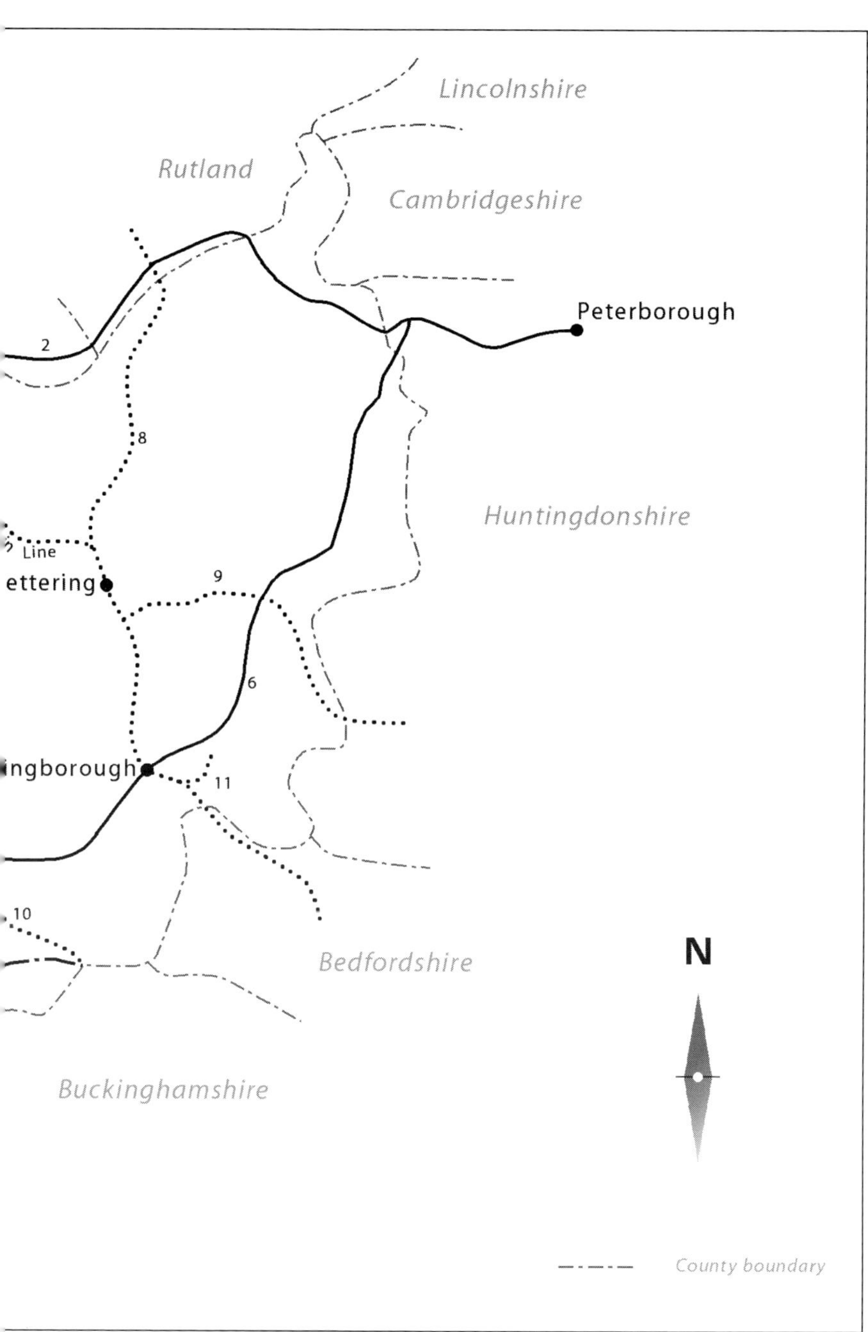

Lincolnshire
Rutland
Cambridgeshire
Peterborough
2
8
Line
ettering
9
Huntingdonshire
6
ngborough
11
10
Bedfordshire
N
Buckinghamshire
County boundary

Introduction

Railways are important in Northamptonshire. But the problem is that the main lines tend to go *through* the county rather than *to* the county. There are hardly any termini in Northamptonshire. One passenger station that was a terminus, Higham Ferrers, only achieved that status because the original plan of a through route to Raunds was never implemented.

Northamptonshire's destiny, therefore, seems to be that of a thoroughfare. It is in the middle of England, and it is also the English county that is bordered by the greatest number of other counties.

Four big railway companies – the London & North Western Railway (LNWR), the Midland Railway (MR), the Great Western Railway (GWR) and the Great Central Railway (GCR) – had north-to-south main lines passing through Northamptonshire, all running to different London termini. The lines of the first three are all still operational today. The exception is the Great Central, the lost main line that is the subject of our first chapter. All the other lost lines in Northamptonshire were local lines.

A significant geographical feature of Northamptonshire is that its two major rivers, the Nene and the Welland, run from west to east. Both these rivers created wide valleys, and these valleys were utilised for two of the most important of our lost lines, the Rugby to Stamford line (which followed the Welland) and the Northampton to Peterborough line (which followed the Nene).

Because of its thoroughfare role and its central location Northamptonshire, even before the motor age, was a county rich in roads. This meant that when the railways came they needed a higher proportion than usual of level crossings. This was not so much of a problem in the 19th century, when road traffic was sparse, and labour, in the form of crossing keepers, was cheap. Road traffic was growing throughout the first half of the 20th century, but the significant event was the abolition of petrol rationing in 1950. This coincided with a spurt in personal incomes, which meant that private car ownership became widespread. In the second half of the 20th century, with that exponential increase in the numbers of cars, lorries and buses using the roads, the high proportion of level crossings in Northamptonshire became a real headache for the railway companies. Road users were now becoming impatient, and angrily intolerant of hold-ups caused by level crossings. At the same time the crossings were becoming more and more expensive to maintain (the growth in personal incomes meant higher labour costs for British Railways). A high proportion of level crossings on a line was often a factor when closure decisions were being taken.

The three surviving main lines are not described in this book, for they are by no means lost – indeed, they have never been busier than in this 21st century. But it is impossible to understand the Northamptonshire railway picture without reference to them, since most of the lost lines fed into them. We therefore summarise them here.

Main line railways were first introduced to Northamptonshire by an enterprise called the London & Birmingham Railway Company (L&BR). The London & Birmingham, true to its name, aimed to provide a direct connection between England's two biggest cities. The line was surveyed and created in the first decade of passenger railways, the 1830s, and it is still there today, sweeping through western Northamptonshire, but missing the county town. It used to be believed that there was initial hostility in Northampton town itself to these new-fangled railways, and that is why the L&BR route did not come through the town. Modern railway historians, however, have shown that this is a myth. The problem was the topography. Northampton town is in a valley, and is 120 feet lower than Blisworth, which was the closest the L&BR came. This had caused problems in an earlier transport revolution. When the Northampton Arm of the Grand Union Canal was made from Gayton (near Blisworth) into the town, it required 17 locks, including ten in one series.

Robert Stephenson, son of the great George Stephenson and already an experienced engineer and surveyor in his own right, though aged only 27 at this period, was brought in to oversee the building of the L&BR. He was determined to have no gradient steeper than 1:330. Locomotives in that early period could not easily handle going uphill. Robert Stephenson is reputed to have said that it would be easy to get trains down into Northampton, the problem would be getting them up out again.

The L&BR line is today part of the West Coast Main Line, one of the most heavily used routes on our passenger network. All the Northamptonshire passenger stations that were on the original line have now closed. Roade was announced as the station for Northampton when it opened on 2 July 1838, even though the

Roade station in the 1930s, looking north. (Stations UK)

Althorp Park station in 1959. It was an imposing building, because it was then the station for Althorp House, the residence of the Earls Spencer and for a short while the home of the young Princess Diana. However, the station closed in 1964 and Long Buckby had to be used instead. (H.C. Casserley)

village of Roade was 6 miles south of the county town, on the old Northampton to London road (today the A508). So a first-class station was built at Roade, but it lost its importance when the Northampton & Peterborough branch (see Chapter 6) was opened in 1845 and trains could run into Northampton itself from Blisworth. By 1862 Roade's refreshment room had been removed, and there were only seven stopping trains a day. But after 1875 LNWR doubled the route capacity to four tracks, and an opportunity was taken, at long last, to use two tracks as a direct main line link into the county town (locomotives were now much more powerful and took uphill climbs in their stride). This link is known as the Northampton Loop. The additional tracks deviate from the L&BR line at Roade, run into Northampton and out again, and re-join it near Rugby. So, at long last, the town of Northampton was on a main line.

With Roade becoming a junction, the station was extended to three platforms, and survived until 7 September 1964. Other stations in Northamptonshire on the L&BR line that have also closed are Blisworth, Weedon and Welton. On the Loop line Church Brampton, Althorp Park and Kilsby & Crick stations have closed, but two stations are still open, Northampton itself and Long Buckby. The latter had its moment of sad fame in 1997 when the mourners attending the burial of Princess Diana were brought here prior to her burial in the grounds of nearby Althorp House.

The second surviving main line is the Midland line. One of the forerunners of the Midland Railway (MR), the Midland Counties Railway, had considered routing its early London connection via Northampton but decided on Rugby instead, probably because of the easier route. The MR finally came into Northamptonshire in the 1850s when it built its line from Leicester to Hitchin in Bedfordshire, from where it had running rights into London King's Cross. This railway was also routed well away from the county town, running to the east of it, but at least it served two other important Northamptonshire towns, Kettering and Wellingborough. Later the MR was to build its own lines south from Hitchin and open its own London terminus, St Pancras. In Northamptonshire itself there were a number of village stations on the Midland line (Irchester, Finedon, Isham & Burton Latimer, Glendon & Rushton and Desborough & Rothwell) but they have all closed; Kettering and Wellingborough, however, remain open.

The Great Western Railway (GWR) is the most surprising company to enter Northamptonshire, since the East Midlands county is a long way from the GWR's normal strongholds of Bristol and Gloucester. But the GWR had reached Oxford, and from there it created a line to Banbury cutting across the south-west corner of Northamptonshire. This line was built originally to the broad gauge (7 ft $\frac{1}{4}$ in), then, after only four years, converted to mixed gauge, and finally to standard gauge (4 ft 8½ in). King's Sutton station, on this line, is still open, the other, Aynho, having closed.

At the peak of railways there were 92 stations in Northamptonshire; today there are only four: King's Sutton, just mentioned; Kettering and Wellingborough on the former Midland line; and Northampton on the Northampton Loop.

In this *Lost Railways* series we do our best to avoid railway jargon. We do, however, find it impossible to avoid using the terms 'up' and 'down', particularly in reference to station platforms. To a railwayman 'up' always means towards London, and 'down' away from London. Another unavoidable term is 'Grouping'. Railways were built in the 19th century by a variety of different companies. On 1 January 1923, all these companies – more than a hundred of them – were brought together by Government edict into four large companies in a process known as 'Grouping'. These survived until nationalisation in 1948, when there was just a single railway organisation, British Railways (later British Rail). The modern privatisation era, in which operating companies bid for franchises, is outside the scope of this book.

Imperial weights and measures have been used throughout. The only unit of measurement that may be unfamiliar to some modern readers is the 'chain'; in railway usage lengths of track are always quoted in miles and chains. A chain is 22 yards, the distance between wickets in cricket.

In the chapter arrangement that follows, the lost lines are described in order of geographical location, working approximately west to east, north to south. I have taken the boundaries of the county of Northamptonshire as they were in 2007. In the 19th century the area known as the Soke of Peterborough was theoretically considered part of Northamptonshire (although it always had a certain independent authority), but is now in Cambridgeshire.

As far as possible my companions and I have tried to follow the routes of the old lines whenever there was a footpath or other legal access. These companions are my brother-in-law Rodger Smith, who came with me on nearly every expedition, my wife Judy and my son Laurence, who both came when they could. In planning our trips we used two sets of Ordnance Survey maps, the modern Explorer series (2½ inches to the mile) and the 'historic' 1905 (1 inch to the mile). The former are excellent in showing where there are still traces on the ground of 'Dismantled Railway'. The 1905 maps, available from the Ordnance Survey, were issued when the railway network was at its maximum. They are useful where there is no longer any obvious evidence on the ground. Ordnance Survey grid references are stated in square brackets, eg '[GR: 993787]'.

Halfway through my work on this book I discovered an extra planning tool that has proved invaluable, the Google Earth internet programme. Not only can the remains of old railways be traced across the landscape, but by changing between distant or close-up views one can examine whether there is anything still on the ground that would be worth a visit.

Geoffrey Kingscott

1
The Great Central Railway

Part of Woodford Yard in 1946. (H.C. Casserley)

The Great Central Railway (from Manchester and Sheffield to London Marylebone) was the last main line to be built in England, and it was intended to be a line for the future. Everything was designed for fast running. Curves, where unavoidable, were kept as shallow as possible, and heavy engineering work was undertaken on cuttings and tunnels, overbridges and underbridges, to ensure there were no level crossings, even for farm access tracks.

Like the LNWR's London to Birmingham main line, the route of the GCR comes down through western Northamptonshire, well away from the town of Northampton itself. It enters the county just south of Rugby. A watercourse called Rains Brook here forms the county boundary, and the line crosses this on an embankment. It

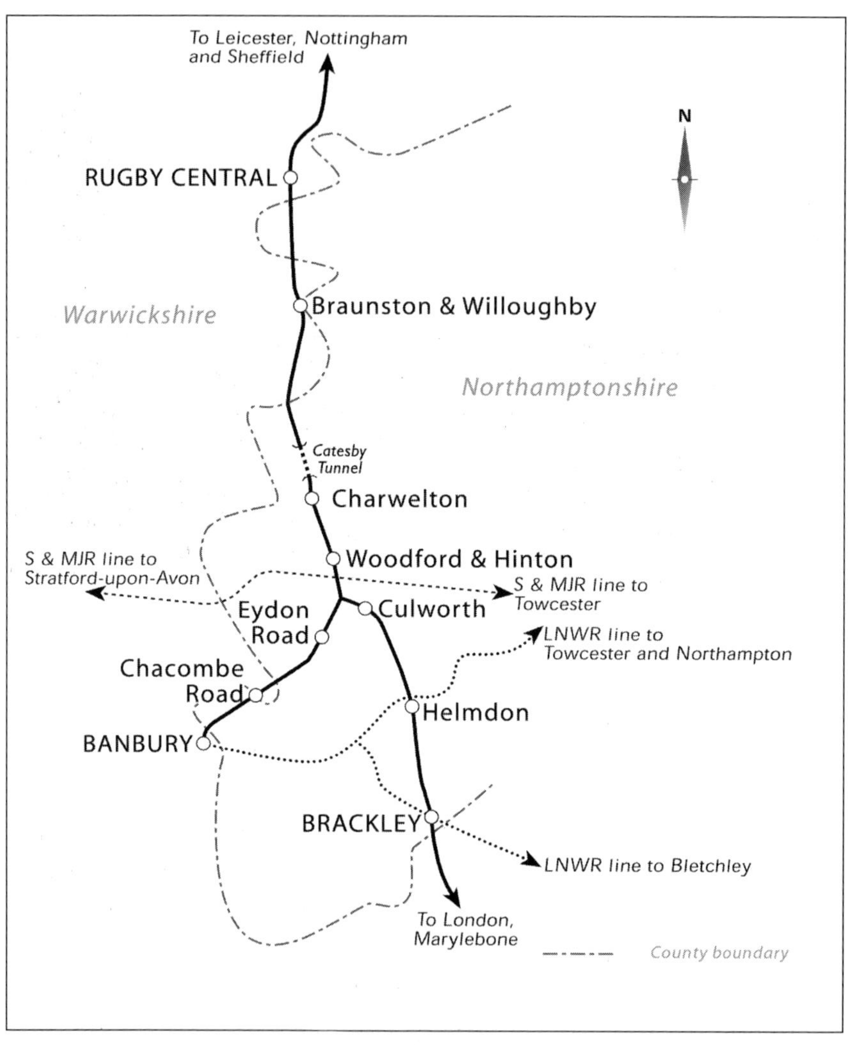
To Leicester, Nottingham and Sheffield
N
RUGBY CENTRAL
Warwickshire
Braunston & Willoughby
Northamptonshire
Catesby Tunnel
Charwelton
Woodford & Hinton
S & MJR line to Stratford-upon-Avon
S & MJR line to Towcester
Eydon Road
Culworth
LNWR line to Towcester and Northampton
Chacombe Road
BANBURY
Helmdon
BRACKLEY
LNWR line to Bletchley
To London, Marylebone
County boundary

Catesby Viaduct today. (Laurence Kingscott)

then passes back into Warwickshire, running parallel to the Oxford Canal for 1¼ miles. Braunston & Willoughby station was just inside Warwickshire, midway between the Warwickshire village of Willoughby and the Northamptonshire village of Braunston. Having crossed the former LNWR Weedon to Leamington line (see Chapter 3) at Wolfhampcote the railway comes definitively back into Northamptonshire west of Staverton.

Here the builders of the line faced major engineering obstacles. They first had to cross two valleys, one of a tributary of the River Leam and the other of the River Leam itself, and then penetrate a range of hills.

The crossing of the valleys required the construction of two viaducts, Staverton Viaduct and the even more impressive 159 yard long Catesby Viaduct, with its 12 semi-circular arches 34 feet in height, in Staffordshire blue bricks. Staverton Viaduct was demolished shortly after the railway was closed, but Catesby Viaduct is still there.

The range of hills that now had to be crossed is the highest in Northamptonshire. It might have been possible to carve a deep cutting between hills, but the owners of nearby Catesby House did not want to see trains, or the smoke of the locomotives, from their windows. They insisted on a tunnel, and so the remarkable structure called Catesby Tunnel had to be excavated. At 2,997 yards (nearly 1¾ miles) it was the longest anywhere on the whole of the GCR main line.

Having insisted on the tunnel the Catesby House owners continued their unreasonableness by not allowing any shafts to be sunk anywhere within the confines of their property, an extensive park. This meant that the builders, for the first 500 yards, had to excavate horizontally. The tunnel was lined, like the viaduct, with Staffordshire blue bricks, and 30 million of them, more than for the Harringworth Viaduct (see Chapter 8), were used in its construction. The tunnel had a reputation for water seeping down, and sometimes cascading onto footplate crews.

A footpath from Upper Catesby to Lower Catesby, past the back of Catesby House, goes over the top of the north portal of the tunnel. This portal is difficult to access (it means clambering down a steep embankment covered in nettles and brambles). Although a search of the internet will bring up stories, including one as recent as 2004, of intrepid adventurers making their way through the tunnel, the entrance is now firmly closed off by a metal grille and a faded sign: 'Danger: Keep Out: Structure Unsafe'. The tunnel itself appears very waterlogged.

David Ablitt of Nottingham walked through the tunnel with a friend in May 1985. It was part of a series of expeditions in the course of which he walked the whole of the line from Annesley in Nottinghamshire to Calvert, from which point he rode (with

The north portal of Catesby Tunnel, glimpsed through the heavy undergrowth that now surrounds it. (Laurence Kingscott)

permission) on an empty diesel train that was returning to Aylesbury after servicing, and from thence travelled by train on the section of the line still in service, to Marylebone. He had a tape recorder with him to collect memories of those he met who had worked or travelled on the GCR. His grandfather had worked on the GCR, and David had always considered it an interesting, indeed romantic, line and decided to walk the length of its route while it was still traceable. He had seen with his own eyes what was happening in Nottinghamshire, where railway cuttings were being filled in and embankments destroyed. He noted some curiosities: apple trees on the embankments (perhaps from cores thrown out of windows); raspberries near where there had been signal boxes; lupins on disused station platforms.

South portal of Catesby Tunnel, showing the grille that prevents unwanted visitors from entering. (Laurence Kingscott)

Walking towards the north end of the tunnel the two friends crossed Catesby Viaduct. They noticed that where ballast had been scraped away when the rails were removed, the waterproof membrane had been damaged in many places, and this had allowed deterioration in some of the piers. When they went

Air shaft for the Catesby Tunnel sitting on a mound made from spoil excavated from the tunnel. (Laurence Kingscott)

through the tunnel, it was not fenced off in any way. They wore walking boots and anoraks, and carried torches. At that time the approach to the tunnel was relatively clear of obstructions, though vegetation was starting to grow.

A bridge (which is still there), positioned shortly before the tunnel portal, added to the gloom surrounding the entrance. Although they knew the tunnel was straight, they could not see the south exit from the north portal. It was only after they had penetrated some 70 to 100 yards into the tunnel that they could make out an extremely faint spot of green in the distance. It was wet underfoot, to a depth of from one to two inches. After some 500 yards they came to the first ventilation shaft. This was the largest (about 15 ft in diameter), since it was the one that had to provide ventilation for the long section under Catesby Hall grounds. Our two intrepid adventurers were relieved to find it and see some daylight again. Water was teeming down at this point, but the original tunnel constructors had incorporated into the masonry recesses two downpipes and a sort of gutter that takes the water into a culvert running the length of the tunnel.

As the two went on they passed further ventilation shafts, these somewhat smaller, about 10 ft in diameter. Near the middle of the tunnel they came across a platelayers' hut, about 10 ft square, set into the side wall – the one dry place in the tunnel! When the line was in operation there had been two gangs of platelayers, one working from the north and one from the south, whose working lengths were half in the tunnel and half in the adjoining open-air section. The more our explorers came nearer to the south end, the deeper became the water on the tunnel floor. At first they tried to walk on the narrow ledges of raked-up ballast, but eventually they had to accept simply splashing through the water, which became knee-deep. When they emerged from the south portal they took off their boots and poured out the water from them as if from a jug.

These days a footpath from the south side of Catesby House goes over the top of the tunnel and joins a bridle path to Charwelton, passing several of the air shafts for the tunnel and grassed-over mounds, which were made from tunnel spoil.

The line rose through the tunnel on a gradient of 1 in 176 and emerged to reach its highest point at Charwelton station. This was designed, as so many GCR village stations were, as an island station reached by steps down from a road overbridge. Charwelton was closed in March 1963 and completely demolished, but it had many similarities to Quorn and Rothley stations, which have been preserved as part of the Great Central Railway heritage line in Leicestershire.

Charwelton station was also the terminus for an industrial railway bringing ironstone from quarries at Hellidon. This is the first time in this book that we have met with the iron ore industry, but it will not be the last. The rich deposits of ironstone in Northamptonshire were usually one of the motives for creating

The site of Charwelton station today. (Laurence Kingscott)

railway lines in this county. It is actually in Catesby Tunnel that the geology of the landscape changes from limestone to ironstone.

Near Charwelton there were water troughs 846 yards in length (nearly half a mile). These were laid out between the tracks and supplied with water from nearby tanks. An express locomotive could lower a scoop and take on a considerable quantity of water, thus saving a stop to replenish its supply.

Proceeding south, the line went between the two neighbouring villages of Woodford Halse and Hinton. At Woodford Halse the GCR built a major locomotive depot with room for up to 30 locomotives (additional space was allowed for future expansion), a turntable, a wagon repair shop and extensive sidings making up a marshalling yard. This made Woodford Halse into one of the two main centres for handling GCR goods traffic (the other was Annesley in Nottinghamshire). The embankment to provide

It is 1946, and the Great Central is now part of the LNER. The 9.10 am Bournemouth to Newcastle train, hauled by locomotive no 4861, leaves Charwelton station. (H.C. Casserley)

a platform for all this working area was provided by some of the spoil from Catesby Tunnel.

When the line opened, on 9 March 1899, the GCR directors rode in an inaugural train from Sheffield to London Marylebone. The parish councillors at Woodford Halse assembled on their station platform intending to deliver an address of welcome and support, but to their surprise the train did not stop. The address had to be sent on by post.

The developments at Woodford Halse brought a wave of newcomers to the tiny village, which was expanded by 200 houses. The population, which was 527 before the coming of the railway, quickly doubled, and by 1931 had reached 1,700, with about half the village's residents estimated to be railway employees. Because of increased freight occasioned by requirements during the Second World War, a second marshalling yard was built in 1941. The yards and depot closed in 1963.

Little trace of the railway yards now remains, and a modern industrial estate occupies part of the site, accessed by a road called Great Central Way. South of here an extensive tract of woodland covers part of the old marshalling yard. The observer will note that the village contains several streets of terraced houses, obviously built at the start of the 20th century to house the influx of railway workers.

The station for this community, reached from the Woodford–Hinton road, was called Woodford & Hinton until 1948, when it was renamed Woodford Halse. The station was an important junction, for just to the south of it, at Byfield, was a connection to the Stratford & Midland Junction line between Towcester and Stratford (see Chapter 7) and then further south, at Culworth junction, a GCR branch line went off to Banbury, where it connected with the GWR main line. Although Woodford Halse had been built in the usual island form, it was found necessary to add an extra platform (reached by a footbridge) for the local services to Stratford and Banbury. The station survived until September 1966. A new housing development occupies the site, which is known as Station Court.

The GCR Banbury line opened in 1900, and stations – actually little more than halts – were opened in 1913 at Eydon Road (serving the village of Thorpe Mandeville) and in 1911 at Chacombe Road (serving the village of Chacombe). These two stations closed in 1956. The route of this line can still be easily traced today until it is sliced through by a more recent change to the landscape: the M40 motorway.

Returning to the GCR main line, the next station going south was at Culworth, which closed on 29 September 1958, the first Northamptonshire GCR main line station to do so. As the station was inconveniently situated over a mile from the small village of Culworth, this was hardly unexpected. Culworth village was actually nearer the Banbury branch, and it is surprising that it did

Terraced houses at Woodford Halse, originally built to house railway workers. (Laurence Kingscott)

not have a station on that railway. Culworth station site (actually closer to the village of Moreton Pinkney than Culworth) is now occupied by farm buildings.

A 9-arch viaduct at Helmdon took the line over a small stream (the infant River Tove) and the Northampton to Banbury line (see Chapter 7). The viaduct is still in place and in good condition.

Helmdon station which was much nearer to the village whose name it bore closed in 1963. It was advertised as Helmdon for Sulgrave, because nearby Sulgrave Manor had associations with the forebears of George Washington, and the idea was to attract American tourists.

The only town (as distinct from villages) in Northamptonshire served by the Great Central Railway was Brackley. The site of the station has now been developed for industrial units, called Top Station Road Industrial Estate (part of it is also called The Sidings), and for housing. The station building is used by one firm, and the old goods shed by another. The closure of the station deprived Brackley of the last of its rail links. Its nearest station is now at Banbury, 8 miles away.

South of Brackley station was one of the line's great engineering structures, Brackley Viaduct, crossing the river known as the Great Ouse. The viaduct was 756 ft long, with 23 arches. The viaduct was demolished in 1978, following problems of vandalism. The landscape has been considerably altered by the enlargement of the A43, which necessitated moving the channel of the Great Ouse. The passage of this river, which formed the county boundary, takes the Great Central line out of Northamptonshire and into Oxfordshire and Buckinghamshire.

The whole Great Central line closed in 1966, but from time to time suggestions are made for the re-utilisation of sections of it, especially south of Rugby, as part of a new north–south route to relieve the congestion on the West Coast Main Line and the East Coast Main Line. There are also schemes for a fast goods-only

The entrance to Woodford Halse station in 1966. (H.C. Casserley) Contrast it with the next picture. Even the letterbox has gone.

Bricked up today, this was where in former times the steps led up to Woodford Halse station. (Laurence Kingscott)

Culworth station in 1958, looking south. (H.C. Casserley)

Helmdon Viaduct. (Rodger Smith)

Helmdon station in 1959, showing something of its carefully-tended flowerbeds and whitewashed stones. It also demonstrates how many GCR stations were built to a pattern. The buildings and the layout are practically identical to those shown in the picture of Culworth. (Stations UK)

Brackley Central station frontage in 1958. (H.C. Casserley)

Brackley station buildings today, used by a car components company, but still very recognisable. (Laurence Kingscott)

At the back of Brackley station buildings there was a footbridge and flights of steps to get down to the platforms. These were demolished when the station was closed and this area is now an industrial estate. (Lens of Sutton)

The date is 31 May 1966, and locomotive 45333 arrives at Brackley Central with the 4.38 pm express from Marylebone to Nottingham. The Brackley station goods shed can be seen to the right of the picture. (H.C. Casserley)

The goods shed today, though the building is now (erroneously) called The Engine Shed, in the middle of an industrial estate, but attractively restored and used by a security company. (Laurence Kingscott)

The last day of service on the Great Central line, and a Class 5 heading a passenger train has just emerged from the Catesby Tunnel. (Derek Huntriss)

route, again on a north–south axis, and the old GCR alignment does have attractions because of a landscape already in place. The most persuasively-argued scheme is that of Central Railway plc (www.central-railway.co.uk). The advantages of such a scheme are so obvious that residents along the route, alarmed that it might well become a reality, have set up the National Central Railway Action Group (NatCRAG) to co-ordinate opposition to it.

2
The LNWR Rugby to Peterborough Line

How it used to be. H.C. Casserley took this picture of the 1.20 pm to Peterborough entering King's Cliffe station on 29 May 1937.

This is a lost line for five counties, for it runs along the boundary between Northamptonshire on the one hand, and – successively – Warwickshire, Leicestershire, Rutland and Cambridgeshire, on the other. The line weaves in and out of county boundaries because – in order maintain an even contour – it is following the two rivers that form those boundaries. It firstly follows the Avon, which flows from east to west, and then picks up the infant Welland, which, flowing eastwards, soon becomes a major river with a wide valley.

Just before it merged with other companies in what was to become the LNWR, the London & Birmingham Railway had decided to follow up the success it had had with its main line which, as already noted, is now known as the West Coast line.

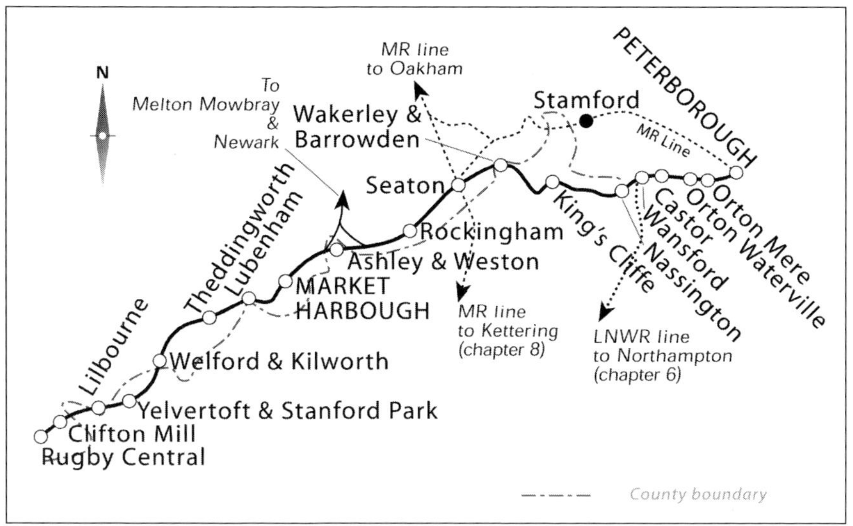

This follow-up idea entailed a west-to-east line from Rugby, via Market Harborough, to Stamford and Peterborough. The line was opened in stages between 1850 and 1852. At first single-line, it was doubled in July 1878.

Part of the impetus behind the building of the line had been to keep the Midland Railway out of Northamptonshire. But at first the LNWR, as it now had become, only got as far as Seaton, from where it had to build forward to a junction with the MR's Syston to Peterborough line at Luffenham in Rutland. For the next 27 years, it had to use that MR line to get to Peterborough. It was not until 1879 that the LNWR managed to build its own line from Seaton to Yarwell junction, giving it at last independent access to Peterborough. This final section was a difficult line to build, since it could no longer use the valley of the River Welland but had to rise over higher ground.

Intermediate stations in the first, earliest, section, between Rugby and Market Harborough, were at Clifton Mill, Lilbourne, Yelvertoft & Stanford Park, Welford & Kilworth, Theddingworth and Lubenham (not to be confused with Luffenham). In the

Rockingham station in 1959, photographed from the Stamford direction. (H.C. Casserley)

Castle Inn, Caldecott, with the route of the trackbed still clearly evident to the right. (Rodger Smith)

second section they were at Ashley & Weston, Rockingham and Seaton, and between Seaton and Yarwell junction they were at Wakerley & Barrowden, King's Cliffe and Nassington.

Because of the weaving in and out of the boundaries, the county situation is complex. Clifton Mill, like Rugby, is definitely in Warwickshire. Lilbourne village is in Northamptonshire but its station was just north of the Avon, and therefore in Leicestershire. The villages of Yelvertoft and Stanford-on-Avon were south of the river, in Northamptonshire, and this time so was their joint station. The Welford & Kilworth station was actually at North Kilworth, well inside Leicestershire, and 2½ miles (nearly an hour's walk) away from Welford village, which is in Northamptonshire. Even more confusingly this station was at one time called Welford & Lutterworth, although the Leicestershire town of Lutterworth was 5 miles to the west. Theddingworth village and station are in Leicestershire. Lubenham is in Leicestershire, but is a border village, adjacent to the infant River Welland, which here takes over from the Avon the role of dividing line between counties. Ashley and Weston-by-Welland villages were south of the river, and so in Northamptonshire, and so too was their joint station – just. Rockingham is a Northamptonshire village, but villagers had to walk north out of their village, and out of their county, to get to Rockingham station (which was strictly speaking in the Rutland village of Caldecott). Seaton is in Rutland. Wakerley and Barrowden were adjoining villages situated in Northamptonshire and Rutland respectively, with their joint station in Northamptonshire – once again, just, because the River Welland flowed close by the station buildings. Then, as mentioned, the line turned away from the river and into the hills, and King's Cliffe, Nassington and Yarwell junction are all well within Northamptonshire.

At one time this line carried long distance boat trains from Birmingham to Harwich, but local passenger traffic was always disappointing. Rural lines like this one began to suffer after the First World War. There was a surplus of motor lorries from wartime use, and these were sold off cheaply. Ex-soldiers who had been trained as drivers by the Army often used their gratuities to buy these lorries and start up local cartage businesses, which competed with the railway. Other ex-Army drivers took to driving the buses that also became part of the post-war scene. Buses could go through the centre of villages, whereas too many railway stations were inconveniently situated well away from the village. The early railway surveyors had paid scant attention to the convenience of passengers, being more interested in maintaining a constant gradient and having space for sidings.

Ashley & Weston station was the first to close to passengers, in June 1951, with Clifton Mill following in April 1953, and Nassington in July 1957. The Beeching Report of 1963 scheduled the whole line for closure, and accordingly remaining passenger services were withdrawn, and stations closed, in June 1966. Welford & Kilworth station was demolished, and its site is now occupied by industrial premises.

Ashley Station House, now a private residence, includes the stationmaster's house and the old waiting room and ticket office. When this station was in full operation, it carried a lot of farm produce. A large loading shed stood in the yard and was used for sacks of corn and other crops. Ashley was also notable as a place for loading cattle, and there were cattle pens adjoining the station. There were a number of stories of cattle escaping and causing mayhem on the line. The rural theme was continued by a public house (now also converted to a private house) called the Graziers' Arms, which stood opposite the station.

Rockingham station, more than a mile from Rockingham, was where the busy A6003 road crossed the railway by a level crossing. Today this road, which has a long history as a trunk road (in the 19th century it was the Nottingham to Kettering

Lilbourne station in 1965, seen from the Market Harborough end. The bridge in the background is carrying the then new M1 motorway. (H.C. Casserley)

The overgrown platforms at Lilbourne station [GR: 562778] can still be seen. (Rodger Smith)

The plaque on Ashley Station House, now a private residence. (Rodger Smith)

turnpike), is so busy with lorries and cars that it is difficult to imagine it being closed for an instant by a level crossing. The Castle Inn at Caldecott, which is still there, was directly opposite the station, and was used by visitors to the station. It is named after Rockingham Castle, which has dominated the village of Rockingham for nearly a thousand years.

At Wakerley the stationmaster's house and altered station buildings still exist, as private residences. King's Cliffe was noted for its wood-turning industry, and local people welcomed the coming of the railway for transporting their products. The station site is now a car park, and leading from it are steps (look out for a

Welford & Kilworth station in April 1965. (H.C. Casserley)

Wakerley & Barrowden station buildings, now much altered, with the stationmaster's house. (Judy Wheldon)

The former stationmaster's house at King's Cliffe; it is now a private residence. (Judy Wheldon)

Steps down to the trackbed from the car park now occupying the site of King's Cliffe station. (Judy Wheldon)

The railway bridge at King's Cliffe. A walk, starting at the former King's Cliffe station, goes over the bridge (Judy Wheldon)

sign to 'Willow Walk') that take one on to the trackbed. Westwards this quickly leads to an industrial estate, but eastwards it goes for some distance, passing over a bridge straddling the King's Cliffe to Wansford road. Beneath the embankment the stationmaster's house – 'Station House' – is still intact as a private residence.

The line came through Nassington on a high level. Nassington station closed in July 1957, nearly ten years before most of the other stations on the line. The station buildings are now a private residence. The abutments of a railway bridge can still be clearly seen north of the village. In October 1912 the station suffered a devastating fire that destroyed one side of it. According to today's village website, only the prompt arrival of Colonel Proby's private steam fire engine from nearby Elton Hall may have saved the whole of the station buildings.

Yarwell junction, where the LNWR's Rugby to Peterborough

The new buildings at what is now Yarwell Junction station on the Nene Valley Railway, Northamptonshire's leading heritage line, seen under construction in 2007. (Judy Wheldon)

and Northampton to Peterborough lines met, is now seeing a new station being erected, to be the new western terminus for the Nene Valley heritage railway, which we shall look at in more detail at the end of Chapter 6.

3
The LNWR Branch from Weedon to Leamington Spa

Weedon station, photographed on its last day in service, in September 1959.
(Stations UK)

By 1803 the Northamptonshire village of Weedon was the central small arms depot for the British Army. It was also the location for a large military barracks. So strategically important was this complex that it had its own branch of the Grand Union Canal. This branch came into the depot under a portcullis, which – as in a medieval castle – could be lowered in an emergency. Because the barracks and depot were considered a safe haven, situated as they were in the centre of the country, it was planned that if Napoleonic troops landed in the south of England the King (George III) and members of the Royal Family would be sent

47

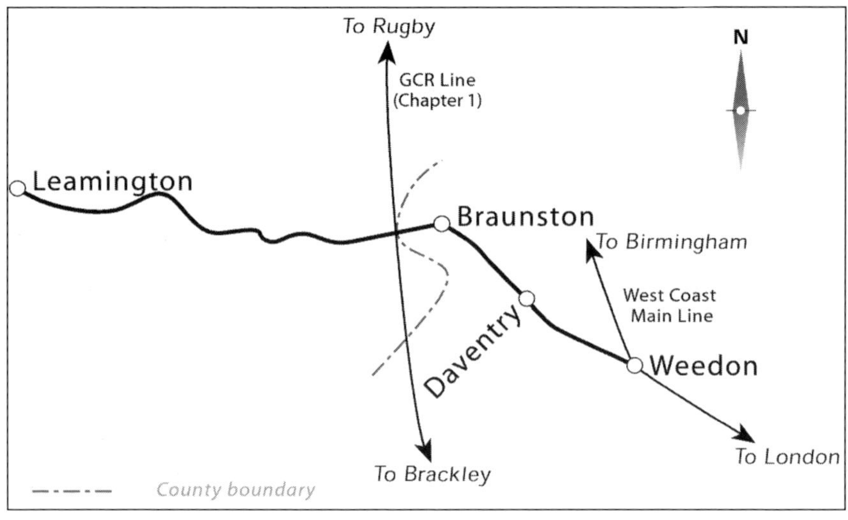

by canal from London to Weedon. Three large pavilions were specially built to house the court.

In the 1830s, when the London & Birmingham Railway was being planned, Weedon was still considered an important port of call in its own right. As with the canal, a special branch was made from the main line into what was then known as the Royal Military Depot. The main line crossed the canal arm by a bridge, which was originally designed to be slid aside to let canal traffic pass. Later the heights of both line and bridge were raised to avoid this awkward arrangement.

As we saw in the Introduction, the L&BR line is today the West Coast Main Line. But Weedon was also the starting place for a lost line to Daventry and Leamington Spa.

Daventry, an important market town in the west of Northamptonshire, still had no rail connection 50 years after the introduction of railway to the county. An independent concern, the Daventry Railway Company, was established to try to meet this lack, but had not been able to proceed. It was not until 1885 that the LNWR obtained the necessary Parliamentary Act to run a

The defensive portcullis over the canal at Weedon Military Depot is still there, even though the canal is no longer used. (Rodger Smith)

branch from its main line at Weedon to Daventry. Weedon station then had to be moved and rebuilt on a larger scale to allow for the extra bay to take the branch line trains. The gradient from Weedon to Daventry rose by 1 in 80, and this part of the line also had sharp curves. This first section of the line opened on 1 March 1888, with the Mayor and Corporation of Daventry travelling to Weedon in a special saloon attached to the first train, the 12.35 pm out of Daventry. The Town Clerk, however, was singled out for special treatment and allowed to travel on the footplate of the engine. The front of this engine was fitted with a Union Jack for the occasion.

Weedon Depot seen from the road. The wooden gates mark the route that the branch leading into the depot would have taken. When we then sought to take photographs from within the depot we were approached and informed this was still Ministry of Defence property and photographing within the precincts was banned. (Rodger Smith)

The exterior of Daventry station in July 1959. (H.C. Casserley)

Braunston station in September 1956, two years before closure.
(H.C. Casserley)

The local newspaper for Daventry, the *Daventry Weekly Express*, is still nicknamed 'The Gusher', which was first applied to a steam locomotive on this line.

In 1890 the LNWR obtained permission to extend the line from Daventry to Leamington Spa in Warwickshire, and this 14-mile extension opened on 1 August 1895. No official ceremonies were held for this opening, but a number of Daventry residents staged their own celebration, walking to Braunston to catch the first return train, back to Daventry. Braunston was the last station in Northamptonshire before the line passed into Warwickshire, and for 60 years enjoyed the luxury of two stations, the other being the Braunston & Willoughby on the Great Central line mentioned in Chapter 1. In consequence the Braunston LNWR station was sometimes called Braunston London Road to distinguish it from the GCR station. It was reached by steps up from London Road

A gradient post from the old railway, showing how steep the line could be, can still be seen at the side of the cycleway. (Rodger Smith)

(today the A45). Braunston must have felt itself to be quite a transport hub, for the village is also at the junction of two of the country's busiest canals, the Grand Union and the Oxford, and in these days of leisure boating it has become a major centre for waterways trades.

The line was single, with passing loops at stations. When it was in full operation a slip coach system was introduced. A slip coach is one that can be uncoupled from an express train without the express stopping. The slipped coach then coasts into the station, and is brought to a standstill by its own braking system. In this instance the coach was slipped from the London to Liverpool express service on the West Coast line, then ran into Weedon station, where it was attached to the Leamington-bound local service.

Not far from Weedon junction the trackbed of the old railway is still intact, as here at Dodford, where it crosses a country lane. (Rodger Smith)

A steam railcar was tried out for two months in 1906 but the gradient was too much for such a vehicle. The LNWR now found it was paying the penalty for having economised when building the line, when it sought to avoid creating steep cuttings or high embankments by accepting steeper gradients. In 1910 a pull and push service started operating, with a two-coach train, and this was the normal pattern until the branch, with all its stations, was closed in September 1958. Daventry, with a population of over 22,000, was then left without any rail link.

Although the rails have long gone, much of the Northampton-shire length of the trackbed survives, except for a section in Daventry itself. There it has been swept away by improvements to the A425 trunk road, and the site of Daventry railway station is now shared by a petrol station and a Macdonald's restaurant.

However, just north of a major roundabout (the junction of the A425 with the A4256 and the B4036), the A425 diverges again from the line of the old railway, a section of which has been turned into a footpath and cycleway. There are hopes that the footpath and cycleway can be extended all the way to Braunston, using trackbed which is still more or less intact. This is one of the schemes taken up as a potential development by Sustrans, the national sustainable transport organisation, and it is one of their reserve schemes. This means that if projects already in their budget have to be withdrawn, as is sometimes the case, they will be able to support the Braunston plan. Councillor Janet McCarthy, chairman of Braunston Parish Council and a member of the Daventry District Council, told us that the residents of Braunston were united in backing the idea. It would benefit the

Footpath and cycleway in north Daventry, created using the embankment of the old railway. (Rodger Smith)

village, which was developing as a tourist locality. It would also be a wonderful alternative to the busy A45 road. In addition to the benefit to cyclists and walkers, it could also encourage plants and wildlife, and develop as a linear park. The scheme is also supported by the West Northamptonshire Development Corporation.

A model of the old Daventry station is now the principal exhibit of the town's archive room in Daventry Town Council offices. This model, remarkable in its detail and in its fidelity to the original, was created by local resident Roger Bignall for a model railway exhibition in 1984, and presented to the Town Council two years later.

At Braunston all trace of the station, which was on the embankment south of the village, has disappeared, but

The last remains of the bridge that once took the railway over the A45 road at Braunston. Apart from this bridge most of the trackbed is still intact. (Rodger Smith)

Roger Bignall's model of Daventry station, now the centrepiece of the museum in the Daventry Town Council offices. (Rodger Smith)

View of the platforms in Roger Bignall's model. (Rodger Smith)

the embankment is still there except for the bridge that once took it over the A45 trunk road. A broad footpath leads from Braunston to the church at Wolfhampcote. This much-visited church has survived intact even though the village it served has long since disappeared. As there are no parishioners, the church has been given a special status and is preserved by the Churches Conservation Trust. The embankment carrying the railway line runs parallel to the footpath, and farm access bridges and a bridge over the River Leam are still in good condition. The railway ran close by the churchyard, but any animation that the trains may have brought has long since disappeared, and the church is once again surrounded by silent fields.

Continuing for about half a mile past the county boundary

Remains of a bridge that once took the Great Central Railway at right angles over the LNWR Weedon to Leamington line. (Rodger Smith)

The famous church for the deserted village of Wolfhampcote seen from the railway embankment (Rodger Smith)

(which here runs along the western wall of the churchyard) brings the walker to the bridge abutments near where the Great Central line crossed the Leamington line at right angles.

4
The LNWR Banbury to Bletchley Line via Brackley

Brackley LNWR station, looking towards Bletchley, in 1955. (H.C. Casserley)

The historic market town of Brackley, in the southernmost part of Northamptonshire, once had two railway stations. But now all the railways have gone.

This is a sad state of affairs for Brackley, which is still a bustling place, serving as a centre not only for its own 9,000 inhabitants but also for a number of rural villages. Its nearest station these days is at King's Sutton, a small village 6 miles away, on the surviving Oxford to Birmingham line (the former GWR line). In pre-railway days Brackley had been an important stop and changing point for stagecoaches, situated as it was at a junction of the road (today's A422) from London to Banbury

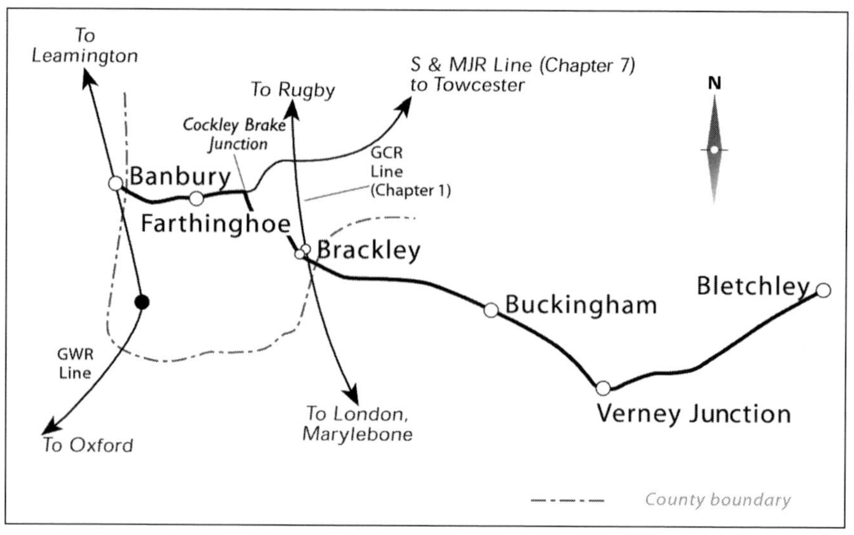

and Birmingham and the road (today's A43) from Oxford to Stamford.

After the London & Birmingham Railway had laid down their main line through Northamptonshire, interest grew in connecting up with towns that lay off the main route. To this end the London & Birmingham encouraged the formation of two companies, the Buckingham & Brackley Junction Railway and the Oxford & Bletchley Junction Railway, which subsequently merged into the Buckinghamshire Railway. Construction started in April 1847 on a line between Banbury and Bletchley, and this opened to passengers on 1 May 1850. The line passed through Brackley, and there was one other Northamptonshire station on the line, at Farthinghoe, a single platform installation.

Banbury station was a modest terminus building, though at one time the LNWR hoped to convert it to a station on a West Midlands through line. But the GWR got in first with their own through line, and their station on the London (Paddington) to Birmingham line was put in alongside the LNWR terminus. As the Buckinghamshire Railway did not have any rolling stock of its own the line was worked from the start by the LNWR, which finally took over the Buckinghamshire Railway in 1857.

When the line first opened there were three passenger trains a day in each direction, but with a vague promise of a more frequent service to come. This, however, was slow to materialise, except for an extra train on Thursdays for Banbury Market. Passenger numbers on the line were low, even when the service frequency did increase. However, there was regular demand for the transport of cattle and sheep to Banbury Market, so much so that cattle trucks were sometimes attached to passenger trains.

Farthinghoe station, awkwardly located a mile from the village whose name it bore, and even though it supposedly served two other villages, Greatworth (2 miles away) and Middleton Cheney (1½ miles away), was always uneconomic. The station was an

The former station house at Farthinghoe, pictured in 1955, looking towards Brackley. In the right foreground can be seen the buffer for the goods siding. (H.C. Casserley)

all-timber construction, but the stationmaster's house in brick was quite imposing. There was a small goods yard with a siding, where cattle and sheep could be loaded. But Farthinghoe was only 3½ miles from Banbury, and from 1930 no longer had its own stationmaster, being controlled from Banbury. Farthinghoe station closed (after almost exactly 100 years of service) in July 1951 to passengers, and October 1951 to goods.

Following the 1955 Railway Modernisation Plan single unit diesel railcars were introduced to the line between Banbury and Buckingham. Passenger numbers improved, but not sufficiently to make the service economic.

Brackley station was sometimes shown on tickets as Brackley Town to distinguish it from Brackley Central on the GCR line. The town itself is on a hill, and Brackley Town station was at the bottom of the hill, to the south, while the GCR station was over a mile away at the top of the hill. Local people, therefore, did not use the names Brackley Town and Brackley Central; they called them Bottom Station and Top Station.

The Bottom Station was in the form of a single loop serving two platforms, with a small goods yard, cattle dock and goods shed. The station buildings were in the attractive yellow-grey stone typical of this part of Northamptonshire. A siding went to the Hopkins & Norris Brewery.

On 13 May 1950 King George VI and Queen Elizabeth, accompanied by Princess Margaret, arrived at Brackley Town station en route to the first official British Grand Prix motor racing event at nearby Silverstone. In 1948 and 1949 Silverstone, a wartime RAF base, had staged unofficial Grand Prix, but the 1950 event was the first round in the first-ever Formula One drivers' championship. It was realised at the last minute that the platform was too low for the Royal Train's exit door, and a box had to be quickly found and upended next to the door. There was no time to cover it with a red carpet, and so the royal

The New Locomotive public house still stands near the site of Brackley Town station. (Judy Wheldon)

personages stepped out onto a wooden box, and from there onto the platform.

A local resident recalled for us how convenient the station was; for a 6d fare one could be in Banbury in a matter of minutes, which was as handy as having to walk up the hill into Brackley town. However, the station closed on 2 January 1961, when passenger services were withdrawn. All the buildings were demolished. The various parts of the site are now occupied by a new road (St James Road), a grassed area, a police station, an industrial estate and residential housing.

The approach to the station from the town of Brackley went in front of a row of cottages on Bridge Street (where the cottages now

The old trackbed south of Brackley Town station still survives, except where it is cut in two by the new Brackley Bypass (the A43). (Judy Wheldon)

have attractive street-side gardens). The bridge, by which the main road crossed the railway, has been demolished, and some of the debris forms the base of the mound that can be seen on the other side of the road. Further along, Pocket Farm Walk uses part of the trackbed. A stroll along Herrieffs Farm Road, which runs parallel to St James Road, will bring you to a set of steps that lead down to the old trackbed. This runs in a straight line until it is severed by the Brackley Bypass (A43), a busy dual carriageway road that is a recent addition to the landscape. Unless you are foolhardy enough to dodge across this road, access to the other side is best achieved by going back into town, and taking Buckingham Road, which will give you access to a footpath along the river. The Great Ouse, though it is the county boundary, seems something of a misnomer at this point, since it is little more than a narrow

Abutments still survive of the bridge that took the line over the Great Ouse river and over the boundary into Oxfordshire. (Judy Wheldon)

Part of the trackbed at Farthinghoe has been turned into a nature reserve. (Laurence Kingscott)

stream. However, we are here only 5 miles from its source, and it is later that the Great Ouse lives up to its name, becoming one of the major rivers of England (and at 150 miles the fourth longest river in the whole of the UK). The footpath mentioned will lead you to where the railway crossed the river by a masonry bridge, the abutments of which still stand. The track can be followed back from here to the south side of the A43.

At Farthinghoe the station site is today occupied by a Waste Recycling Centre. Nothing remains of the station except a plum tree that was formerly in the stationmaster's garden. Railway land nearby is now part of Farthinghoe Nature Reserve. An adjoining meadow was where sheep and cattle were kept before being loaded for transport to Banbury Market.

5
The LNWR Market Harborough to Northampton Line

A locomotive without a train – known in railway parlance as a 'light engine' – running through Lamport station towards Northampton in the 1930s. (Stations UK)

Iron ore and passengers: these were the two principal motives for opening new railway lines in Northamptonshire. And nowhere was this truer than for the line between Market Harborough and Northampton.

It was in 1851 that a large ironstone field was discovered near Brixworth, close to the turnpike road from Northampton to Market Harborough. Both the MR and the LNWR were interested in exploiting the new find, but it was the LNWR that moved the more quickly. And from a passenger point of view the LNWR

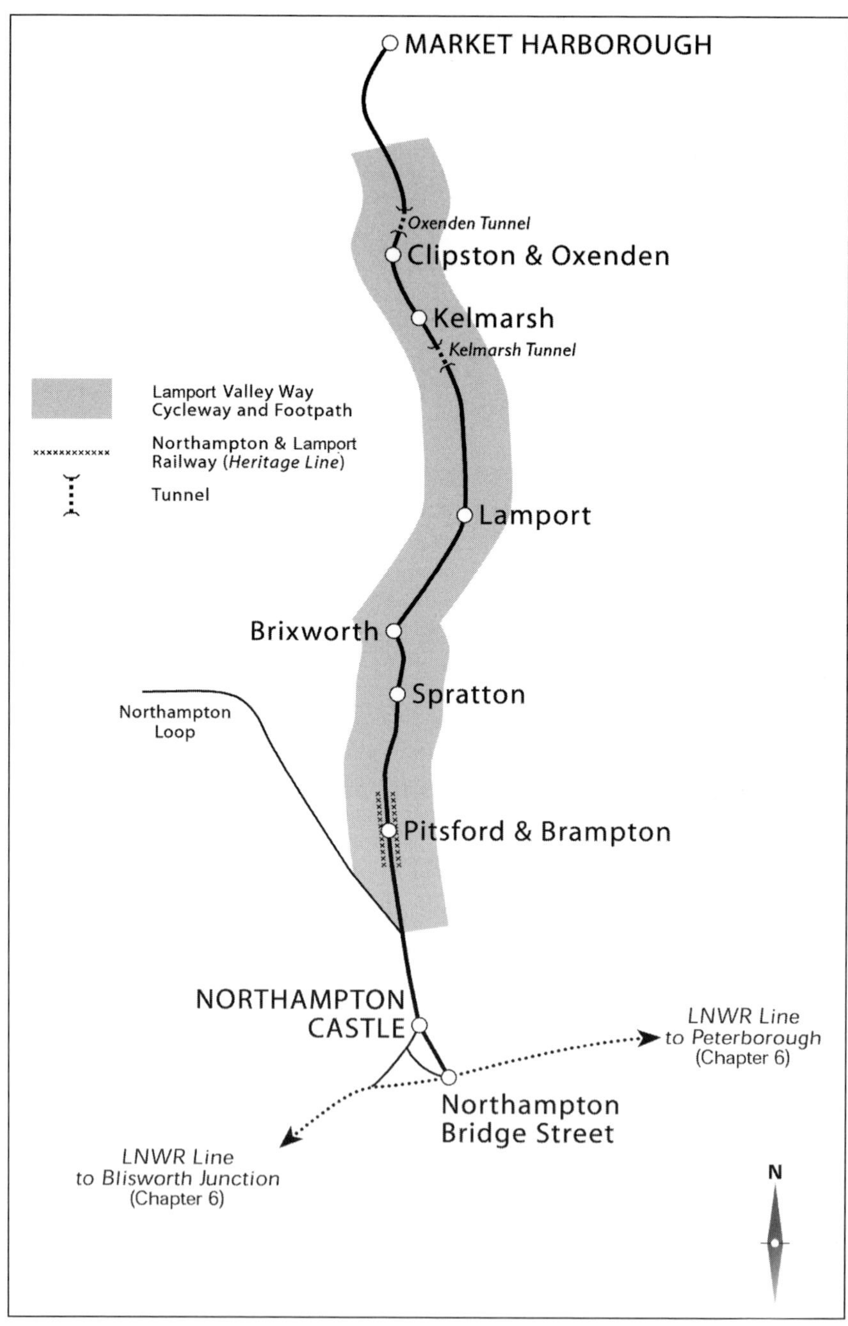

MARKET HARBOROUGH
Oxenden Tunnel
Clipston & Oxenden
Kelmarsh
Kelmarsh Tunnel
Lamport Valley Way Cycleway and Footpath
Northampton & Lamport Railway (Heritage Line)
Tunnel
Lamport
Brixworth
Spratton
Northampton Loop
Pitsford & Brampton
NORTHAMPTON CASTLE
LNWR Line to Peterborough (Chapter 6)
Northampton Bridge Street
LNWR Line to Blisworth Junction (Chapter 6)
N

was also interested in having a north–south line that could link into its two west–east lines, the Rugby-Peterborough line (Chapter 2) and the Northampton–Peterborough line (Chapter 6).

Market Harborough, which is just inside Leicestershire, had been an important coaching centre, and had many links to Northamptonshire. Once again it looked as if the town of Northampton would miss out. In the original plans the line would have left the new Rugby–Peterborough line close to Market Harborough and run almost due south through the western part of Northamptonshire to Blisworth junction, with no provision for a station in the county town itself. Passenger potential then caused the LNWR to have second thoughts, and it announced that it would run northbound trains into its Northampton Bridge Street station (which was built to serve the Northampton to Peterborough line described in Chapter 6), reverse them out again to the junction, and then continue to reverse southwards on to the main line until they were facing Market Harborough. The Inspecting Officer for the Board of Trade indicated that he did not like this arrangement, and the LNWR therefore had to plan for a second Northampton station.

A new station was in place for when the line opened in February 1859, and this was the station that came to be known as Northampton Castle. At that time, however, it was small, and catered only for passengers. Goods were still handled at Bridge Street.

It is necessary to digress here, to explain that when, later, the Northampton Loop from the West Coast Main Line was created, it came through Northampton Castle station. This was by now quite inadequate for such increased responsibilities and something had to be done about it. The LNWR was nothing if not ambitious. Firstly they bought the whole site of the old castle, demolished what was left and cleared the area. Northampton

Castle had been the scene of a number of incidents in English history, and archaeologists today would have a fit at the loss of an area of such significance, but the LNWR's need for expansion swept everything before it. Local antiquarians did express some misgivings, and as a sop to their feeling the one intact feature of the old castle that was still standing in the 1870s, the Postern Gate, was moved to a new site in the boundary wall of the extended station. There it can still be seen, the last forlorn reminder of a major fortress. The goods shed today occupies much of the land where the castle keep used to stand.

That was not all that had to be done to provide for the new station. Arrangements also had to be made to divert the course of the River Nene, which was restricting the western area of the site. When Bridge Street station was closed in 1964, Northampton Castle became the town's only station. It was therefore renamed 'Northampton'. It was extensively remodelled by BR in 1966.

For completeness we should also mention that the increased traffic meant that a new, much larger, Market Harborough station was also created at this time. The new station, jointly owned and run by the MR and the LNWR (though goods facilities were separate) came into operation on 14 September 1884. The buildings on the higher level were of a mundane design, but the street-level station entrance was an imposing structure in Queen Anne style, which is today recognised as an architectural gem.

Returning to the history of the Market Harborough to Northampton line, the actual route was designed by George Bidder and George R. Stephenson, a nephew of Robert Stephenson. Stations on the line, from south to north, were Northampton Castle, Pitsford & Brampton, Spratton (opened in 1864, as a result of the villagers' request), Brixworth, Lamport, Kelmarsh, Clipston & Oxenden (opened in 1863, again as a result of the villagers' request), and Market Harborough. All but the latter were in Northamptonshire.

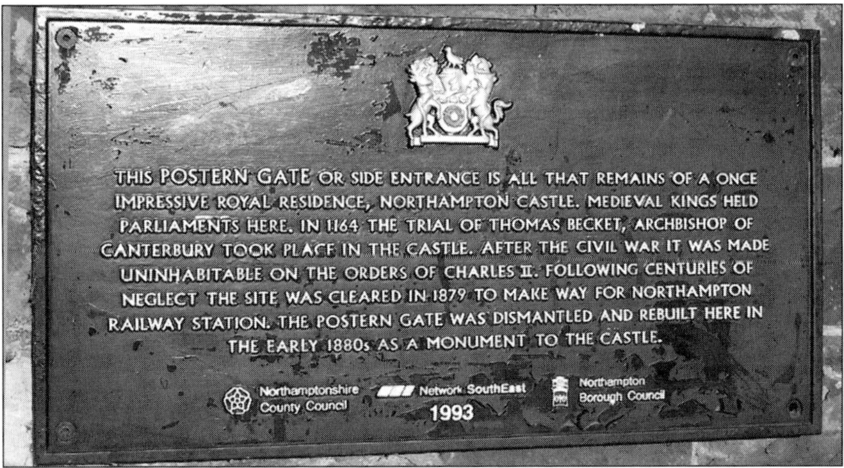

The Postern Gate, the only relic of Northampton Castle, on its new site near Northampton station, and a closer view of the plaque, which records some of the castle's history and the clearance of the site to make way for the railway station. (Rodger Smith)

In order to maintain an even gradient, the line ran mostly along a valley, but the villages were on the ridges each side of the valley. Not one of the stations, therefore, was conveniently situated for residents in the communities along the line. In the 19th century this was a matter of no importance: no one thought it a problem to have to walk a mile or two to the nearest railway station. But in the 20th century it had the result of making the line, as with so many rural lines, unable to compete for convenience with the motor bus, which stopped in the village centre.

The line, which opened without ceremony, was 18 miles 29 chains in overall length. A typical journey, end-to-end, in the early days would take 50 minutes.

The Vicar of Brixworth, the Rev C.F. Watkins, appears to have been a man of energy and wide interests, and he was a prime mover not only in suggesting (complete with maps) a site for Brixworth station, but also, in 1863, in developing the first ironstone workings along the line, Brixworth Old Pits. The line was made single-track, but bridges over the line were built wide enough to allow for later double-track. But, because of the cost, the two tunnels were only single-track, which meant that expensive extra tunnel bores had to be executed when the decision was made to double.

A landslide at the north face of Kelmarsh Tunnel delayed the opening of the line for nearly a year, but the first passenger train ran on 16 February 1859. By the late 1860s there were four passenger trains a day in each direction, and one iron ore train a day in each direction.

It was the increase in goods traffic that made it necessary to go to double-track. This increase was the result of opening up of additional iron ore mines, and also coal coming in from the Nottinghamshire and Derbyshire coalfields after the completion of the joint LNWR/Great Northern line from Newark to Market Harborough in 1879. That link gave the LNWR access over

Locomotive 48656 at the head of a goods train leaving Pitsford Ironstone Siding in 1958. (R.M. Casserley)

GNR lines both to the city of Nottingham itself and also to the Nottinghamshire and Derbyshire coalfields, some of the most productive in the country. In return the GNR were given running rights over the LNWR's Market Harborough to Northampton route.

The new joint line also brought in more passenger traffic, with direct trains between Nottingham and Northampton, and a through coach from Melton Mowbray North (a station on the joint line) to London Euston. This converted the Market Harborough to Northampton railway from a branch line into a through route.

At Grouping, when both the Midland Railway and LNWR became part of the LMS, their old rivalry ceased to be relevant. This produced much greater flexibility so that trains could be run to and from either Euston, the old LNWR London terminus, or St Pancras, the MR terminus. The LMS reorganised junctions at Market Harborough so that southbound trains on the old Midland line could be sent down the Lamport line and on to Euston, while northbound trains could come out of Euston but switch at Market Harborough on to the old Midland line for destinations further north. After the creation of the Northampton Loop the section south of the junction as far as Northampton itself was quadrupled.

Between the wars the line was busy with both goods and passenger traffic. The passenger trains included expresses, stopping trains and excursions. On Saturdays only in the summer there was a direct train between Northampton and Skegness, a seaside resort much favoured by Midlanders.

Spratton station was closed on 23 May 1949, Pitsford & Brampton on 5 June 1950. Then in December 1953 came the closure of the Newark–Market Harborough line, which had brought in so much through traffic. This also meant the end of the direct Northampton to Nottingham service via that route. In compensation a Northampton to Nottingham service via Market

H.C. Casserley took this picture of Brixworth station from a passing train in 1955.

Harborough and Leicester was introduced. The remaining intermediate stations – Brixworth, Lamport, Kelmarsh, Clipston & Oxenden – were all closed in January 1960. The line remained in place as an alternative route, and in 1969, between January and May, it was used for some diverted St Pancras to Glasgow sleeper trains. It was again opened to through traffic on 10 July 1972, but regular passenger services were finally withdrawn on 26 August 1973. Some excursions continued to use the line for a few more years. After withdrawal of services, but before final closure, the Royal Train was sometimes parked on the line.

In June 1981 a revival group was established, and it was they who organised a special train, on 15 August 1981, from Northampton to Market Harborough and back. It was the last train, passenger or goods, to use the line while it was still part of the national network. People crowded to the lineside to watch. The next day, 16 August 1981, British Rail formally closed the line. In 1982 track realignment at Market Harborough took out the junction with the old MR main line. This means that without some costly reinstatement, even if the line re-opened, it would not regain its role as a through route.

The revival group, which eventually took the name of Northampton & Lamport Railway, set up its headquarters in the old goods yard at the former Pitsford & Brampton station. Their work was expanded to include a station, two signal boxes, ¾ mile of running line, and sidings. The first passengers were carried on 19 November 1995, and on 31 March 1996 crowds gathered on the old platform to watch as a Pecket 0-4-0 saddle tank, no 2104, broke through a banner strung across the track to signify the re-opening of a section of line. Volunteers then worked on phase 2, the extension of the line, and in 2002 the first passenger train crossed what was known as Bridge 13 after its closure by British Rail in 1981. The next phase is a ½ mile extension of the line south to Boughton Crossing, where a run-round loop and station will be built.

A beautifully restored signal box on the Northampton & Lamport heritage railway. (Author)

In 1987 the trackbed of the Market Harborough to Northampton Railway was purchased by the Northamptonshire County Council, with the help of a grant from the Countryside Commission. Now three-quarters of the alignment of the former railway – a 14-mile continuous route – has been made into a footpath and cycleway, called the Brampton Valley Way. This is now part of Route 6 of the Sustrans National Cycle Network. The Brampton Valley Way was officially opened by Lady Hesketh on 8 April at a ceremony at Boughton Crossing. The existence of the Way means that this is the easiest of the lost lines of Northamptonshire to explore.

Going north from Northampton, the Brampton Valley Way starts at Boughton Crossing [GR: 736653], just outside the built-up

A train awaiting departure from the restored Pitsford & Brampton station in the autumn of 2007. Motive power was provided by 31289 Phoenix standing by the signals and D5401 at the rear. The Brampton Valley Way footpath can be seen to the right of the picture. (Rodger Smith)

area of the county town. Within ½ mile, at Bridge 11, is found the southern terminus of passenger services on the Northampton & Lamport Railway. There is room for railway and cycleway to run side by side, as shown in the photograph.

The present northern terminus of the N&LR is just before Bridge 14, a steel girder bridge over a tributary of the River Nene, one of the streams that create the valley. Eventually they hope to extend the line northwards another ½ mile to Merry Tom Crossing, a former level crossing on the line. From Merry Tom Crossing there is a bridle road to Brixworth Country Park, one of the favourite recreational places for people from Northampton. The park, which overlooks the extensive complex of reservoirs

The Brampton Valley Way, seen near Spratton car park. (Rodger Smith)

known as Pitsford Water, not only has a café and several picnic sites but also a major cycle hire centre.

One of the main locations for accessing the line is at the site of the former Spratton station, where a car park and picnic site have been created. The N&LR has long-term plans to rebuild the station.

When the local landowner sold land for the original railway, he demanded as a condition that a station be located by the side of the Market Harborough to Northampton turnpike road. This became Lamport station. Today the turnpike road has become the busy A508, and this is the one place on the 14-mile length of the Brampton Valley Way where walkers and cyclists have to cross a main road. The Lamport Station House still exists, as do some railway cottages.

There is another car park adjacent to the line at Maidwell (a village which never had a station on the line). The line now starts to rise up out of the valley and the landscape becomes more

Kelmarsh Tunnel from the south. (Judy Wheldon)

undulating. A mile north of Maidwell the path goes under the modern A14 and reaches Kelmarsh Tunnel. One of the two bores has now been blocked off, but the other is open to cyclists and walkers – horse riders must take a diversion. Cycling or walking through an old railway tunnel is always an exciting experience. Your author has experienced it on the Rail Trail in New Zealand, and on a specially-arranged walk on the Monsal Trail in Derbyshire shepherded by National Park rangers, but it is rare in our safety-obsessed country for tunnels on a public path to provide free passage. The administrators of the Brampton Valley Way are to be congratulated on their initiative.

The tunnel, about ¼ mile in length, is unlit. Cyclists are

The ventilation shaft of the Kelmarsh Tunnel, seen from below. (Judy Wheldon)

advised to dismount unless they have good lights. Every walker should have a torch, partly to see the tunnel floor (there are wet and uneven patches) and partly so as to be visible to cyclists. Part way along the tunnel daylight can be seen up an impressive ventilation shaft.

Half a mile north of the tunnel is the site of Kelmarsh station, now a car park and picnic site. A public house, the Kelmarsh Arms, was erected near the station, but has long since been a private residence. However, in the gable above the front door, the words 'Kelmarsh Arms 1910' can still be made out.

Steps up to the railway from the car park at the site of Kelmarsh station. (Judy Wheldon)

A house sign in Great Oxenden village, which is self-explanatory in describing its location. (Judy Wheldon)

Clipston & Oxenden station was south of the village of Great Oxenden, close to the Harborough road. A row of houses, called Station Cottages, now indicate the site. In the village of Great Oxenden itself there is the second tunnel on the Brampton Valley Way, very similar to Kelmarsh Tunnel in every way, though slightly shorter. Both sets of tunnels had narrow bores, and were consequently known to generations of engine drivers as 'the ratholes'.

The Brampton Valley Way reaches its northern end at Little Bowden Crossing, where the crossing keeper's house still stands.

6
The LNWR Northampton to Peterborough Line

A 12.50 pm arrival from Peterborough at Northampton Bridge Street station in 1959. (H.C. Casserley)

As mentioned in the Introduction, the London & Birmingham line missed Northampton town for topographical reasons, not because of any hostility on the part of the townspeople. The only fault that can be imputed to the good burghers of Northampton is that they were slow on the uptake, and no one at first thought to protest at this new-fangled railway route missing the town. But once the line was open, and it was clear that railways were going to transform the country's transport system, it was realised what an opportunity had been missed. The introduction of a stagecoach service between

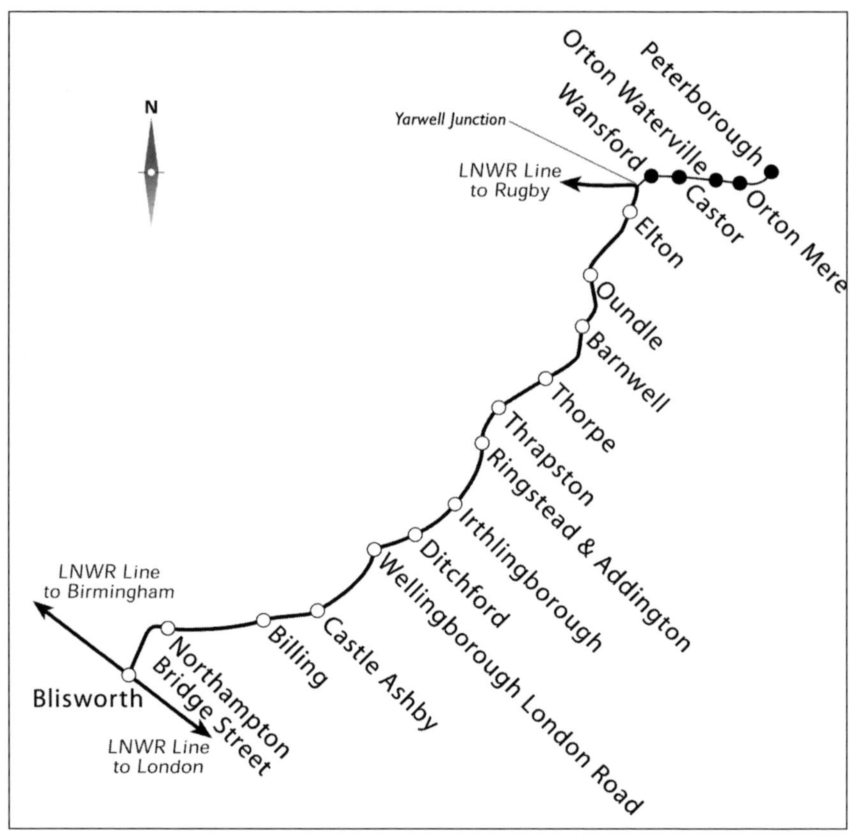

Northampton and Blisworth to provide a connection to the railway had quickly been perceived as quite inadequate. Over 100 of the town's businessmen, from both the Tory and Whig factions, therefore organised a public meeting on 8 March 1838, which resulted in a delegation to meet the L&BR board and plead for a branch into Northampton itself, and for a Northampton station.

The L&BR board was quite willing to listen to the delegation, since they took the view that a line through Northampton and then on to Peterborough, an expanding town, could be profitable. Peterborough was the last downstream point at which the River Nene could be crossed, and had already been made prosperous by the coming of the Great Northern railway's London to York line. It was by now eclipsing nearby Stamford as a commercial and industrial centre.

Since 1839 the 'Victoria', a regular stagecoach had been running between Peterborough and the L&BR station at Blisworth, passing through Oundle, Thrapston, Wellingborough and Northampton, and this gave a clue as to where there was a passenger demand. The proprietors of the 'Victoria' were at least conscious of the need to link up with the railway. A rival company, proprietors of the 'Old Northampton', the stagecoach link between Northampton and London, held out against the new invention, and they put an advertisement in the local paper addressed 'To those Ladies and Gentlemen who prefer the old-fashioned way of travelling as superior to the new', assuring them that 'the "Old Northampton" offers in every respect the safest and best accommodation they can wish for'.

Road improvements between 1810 and 1830 had given a boost to stagecoach travel, the average speed of mail coaches rising from 6.56 mph to 9.45 mph. The desire for greater and greater speed meant that stops, for food, drink and toilet needs, were made shorter and shorter, as coaching inn staff became adept at changing horses quickly. The 'Old Northampton' left the Angel Inn in Northampton every day at 8.45 am, arriving in London at 3.30 pm. But of course for speed and comfort it was quickly clear that the railway would win every time. Within ten years the stagecoach network – which in the 1820s had employed some 30,000 people nationwide – had collapsed, and the only coaches that survived were those which, like the 'Victoria', took passengers to railway stations. And they in their turn disappeared as the railway branches spread through the countryside.

So the L&BR, soon to become part of the LNWR, built the most important of the county's lost lines, a railway which branched from the London to Birmingham main line, went through the middle of Northampton, and then traversed the county from west to east before ending at Peterborough. Centres such as Wellingborough, Irthlingborough, Thrapston, Oundle, Wansford would now have a railway connection, and therefore Northamptonshire in its own right was really on the railway map at last.

As with the London to Birmingham main line, Robert Stephenson was once again in charge, and work started in March 1844. Apart from the initial descent into the town, the line took an easy route, following the valley of the River Nene. However, this valley was also popular with road builders, and this meant a lot of level crossings. The line branched off the original L&BR main line at Blisworth, and was opened as far as Northampton by May 1845. The creation of a junction required Blisworth station to be replaced by a new and bigger one serving the junction. The new line was then quickly completed as far as Peterborough, a total of 47 miles, nine months ahead of schedule. And just one month after that the L&BR was one of several railway companies that merged to form the LNWR. Indeed the LNWR was shortly to become the world's largest joint-stock company, a title it retained through much of the mid-19th century.

The first train to traverse the whole line from Peterborough to Blisworth left at 7 o'clock in the morning of 2 June 1845, using the passing loop at Thrapston to pass the first train from London to Peterborough. When this latter reached Peterborough it was greeted with a brass band and the pealing of bells. On the way there were sightseers at every crossing to cheer it on, or, as the *Northampton Mercury* put it: 'Every station along the line was crowded with gazers, looking with wondering eyes upon the imposing novelty.'

The line was given an early boost when, in 1847, Northampton was home to the Royal Agricultural Show. This was appropriate,

Locomotive 41218 at the head of a train coming off the Peterborough line onto the main line, and about to enter Blisworth station. The date is 24 June 1956. (H.C. Casserley)

because Northamptonshire was a centre for the rearing of cattle for meat, and there was a cattle market in Northampton. The cattle, sent down to Smithfield Market in London, were to become an important source of revenue for the line.

The Great Exhibition of 1851, masterminded by Prince Albert, husband of Queen Victoria, and staged in the spectacular Crystal Palace in Hyde Park in London, gave a major stimulus to rail travel. A large proportion of those who could afford it, particularly from the burgeoning middle classes, became 'excursionists' – one of the new words thrown up at the time. As a company the LNWR did particularly well, running 145 excursions, and conveying 775,000 people into and out of London while the exhibition was open. And what we now think of as Northamptonshire was still exclusively LNWR territory. The Great Northern Railway, which had moderately good relations with the LNWR, was well established in Peterborough; until 1888 the Soke of Peterborough

Blisworth station in 1956. (H.C. Casserley)

was formally part of Northamptonshire, though with certain detached rights. Today Peterborough is an independent unitary authority but part of the ceremonial county of Cambridgeshire.

The station in Northampton, which had been originally just 'Northampton', was renamed Northampton Bridge Street in 1876. Bridge Street station declined in importance after 1881 with the opening of a curve that allowed trains from Blisworth to access Castle station and the Market Harborough line described in the previous chapter. However, it continued to be used until the closure of the Peterborough line in 1964. Now demolished, it was regarded as an architectural gem, being in Jacobean style. Tracks, though overgrown, are still in place, where industrial sidings were in use until 2005.

As our various photographs show, the stations outside Northampton were built in an Old English or Tudor style from local limestone. The original line was made double-track between Blisworth and Northampton, and single-track from Northampton to Peterborough, with a passing loop at Thrapston, which was the halfway point. Although it had not been a major factor in inducing the L&BR to build the line, iron ore was to prove an important source of freight traffic, with quarries opening up to supply new blast furnaces at Wellingborough, Kettering and Corby.

The worst passenger accident on the line occurred on 18 October 1877. A damaged goods train was blocking the down line at Castle Ashby, so an eastbound train from Northampton Castle station, carrying many passengers who had been attending Quarter Sessions in Northampton – judges, lawyers, witnesses and journalists – was switched to the up line. Between Hardingstone junction and Billing it collided head on with a train travelling in the other direction, and there were four fatalities.

In July 1963 BR announced the proposal to withdraw services on the line, which would close except for a freight section between Peterborough and Oundle. The high number of manned level crossings was certainly a contributory factor in the decision, but the main consideration was that emphasised in the Beeching Report of March 1963. This was that stopping train services were uneconomic and should be done away with as far as possible, particularly on rural lines. Regular passenger services ceased 2 May 1964, though specials to Oundle School, a large public school, ran until 1972. But the following stations closed to passengers: the south bays at Northampton Castle station, Northampton Bridge Street station, Castle Ashby, Wellingborough London Road, Irthlingborough, Ringstead & Addington, Thrapston Bridge Street, Thorpe, Barnwell, Oundle and Peterborough East. Billing station closed slightly earlier than most of the others, on 6 October 1952 to passengers and 1 June 1964 to goods. The main station building still stands, though now used for commercial purposes. The platforms have been demolished.

A closer view of the Jacobean-style architecture at Northampton Bridge Street, shown particularly in the elaborate chimney pots. (H.C. Casserley)

The site of Northampton's Bridge Street station today. (Rodger Smith)

A fine example of LNWR station architecture. It is 24 September 1959, and locomotive 62551 has just left Wellingborough London Road station with the 8.35 am Northampton to Peterborough train. (H.C. Casserley)

Crowds gathered to see the last (westbound) train, on 2 May 1964, carrying a wreath on its smokebox. Bus services were substituted, but there were complaints that these were slower or less convenient. Barnwell children were particularly badly affected, since they had been accustomed to take the train to go to the local authority school in Oundle. But Barnwell was within 3 miles of Oundle, and the rule was that the county council could not subsidise travel (ie a school bus) for pupils living within a 3-mile radius of the school. Since Oundle railway station was still being used for special trains for those in private education at Oundle School, this was particularly contentious. Eventually a compromise was found, whereby a school bus was arranged for Barnwell children, but their parents had to contribute to the travel costs.

Wellingborough London Road station has been almost

The 12.40 pm train from Northampton leaves Castle Ashby station on 22 April 1959. (H.C. Casserley)

An earlier picture of Castle Ashby station, from the 1930s, and taken from the opposite direction. Note the sidings to the goods depot on the left of the picture. (Stations UK)

The Castle Ashby goods shed seen in the background of the 1930s photograph has been turned into a restaurant. (Rodger Smith)

completely obliterated, with most of the site under the A45/A509 road improvements. This station was quite separate from Wellingborough's Midland Railway station, which remains to this day a busy station on the Leicester to London main line. There was, however, a spur at Wellingborough linking the LNWR and Midland lines, and this had become more widely used when both the MR and the LNWR became part of the LMS at Grouping. The LNWR station had an important siding for the Little Irchester ironstone mines, which were an important source of freight traffic for much of the line's existence. Occasional goods trains were served by the station until 1982.

At Ditchford the site has been obliterated by the building of an access road to sewage works. A location without any resident population (apart from the stationmaster's family) it was closed for passenger traffic as early as 1 November 1924 but stayed open for freight till 1 May 1950. It was also used by railwaymen and their families till 1952.

The station for Irthlingborough was some distance from the town, on the opposite side of the River Nene, and passengers had to cross an old packhorse bridge to get to it. When it opened the station was known as Higham Ferrers, after the village on the south of the Nene, then renamed as Higham Ferrers & Irthlingborough on 28 April 1885, and finally just Irthlingborough on 1 October 1910. After passenger closure it continued to handle iron ore traffic until 6 July 1966. Near here all that remains are the overgrown remains of loading dock, and rails embedded in the road at the side of the level crossing, though part of the old trackbed route can be walked at Summer Leys Country Park.

There is still a Station Road leading out of the village of Ringstead, and this eventually brings you to the site of Ringstead & Addington station [GR: 970744], closed in May 1964. The station buildings have been completely removed, but a curious piece of railway history can be found alongside the footpath to

Although Ditchford station closed to passengers in 1924, the buildings were still there as late as 1962. (H.C. Casserley)

Great Addington. These are the original stone sleepers used in the earliest days of the line, but later replaced by the orthodox wooden sleepers. Because the footpath, which crosses the River Nene by a footbridge, is often muddy in winter, the sleepers can be used as stepping stones. In summer, however, the stones are covered by long grass and are difficult to see. This station was known simply as Ringstead until 1 April 1898, but then changed to its later names, to include the small villages of Great Addington and Little Addington.

Thrapston's station on this line was known as Thrapston Bridge Street, to distinguish it from the Midland Railway's Thrapston Midland Road station. As well as being a market town in its own right Thrapston was an important centre for cattle, with 15,000 being brought there every year to fatten up for Smithfield Market. The LNWR station was on the north side of Bridge Street. The station remained open for freight until 7 June 1965. No trace of it now remains, and industrial premises occupy the site.

At Thorpe the station buildings are now part of a private residence, with some extensions added. At Barnwell the station house survives as a private residence, and the remains of one platform can also be seen. The main station building, added in 1884, has been re-erected as Wansford station on the Nene Velley Railway. On 14 June 1962, the Queen and Duke of Edinburgh arrived on the Royal Train at Barnwell station to attend the coming of age celebrations for Prince William of Gloucester, and the train was stationed at Barnwell overnight.

After standing derelict for many years, the Jacobean-style station building at Oundle has been renovated as a private residence. The up platform is there but under grass. A housing estate occupies what was the station forecourt. The Oundle bypass is built on a section of the line.

Though Irthlingborough station was inconveniently situated for its town of Irthlingborough, the Northampton platform there looks busy in 1960, only four years before closure. Note again the elaborate architecture of the main station buildings on the left of the picture. (H.C. Casserley)

Ringstead & Addington station in 1954. (H.C. Casserley)

The site of Ringstead & Addington station today. (Judy Wheldon)

Elton station has been demolished. No trace remains apart from a level crossing gatepost. The station was in Northamptonshire but the village of Elton is actually in Huntingdonshire. The reverse applies at Wansford, where the village is in Northamptonshire but the station is 3 miles away, in Huntingdonshire. The county boundary here is the River Nene.

At Yarwell junction [GR: 078970] the line was joined by the Rugby to Peterborough line (described in Chapter 2), and from here on we have a lost line that has been brought back into operation. For Yarwell Junction station is the western terminus of the 7½-mile Nene Valley Railway, one of the country's leading

Old stone sleepers now used as stepping stones alongside a muddy footpath. (Judy Wheldon)

Thrapston LNWR station in 1954. Notice that we have here, as on most of the other stations on this line, a level crossing over a busy road. The high proportion of level crossings was one of the considerations that led to the decision to close the line. (H.C. Casserley)

heritage lines. From Yarwell Junction the line crosses under the Elton road, the B671, using the Wansford Tunnel.

BR closed the Northampton to Peterborough line in 1972. But an organisation called the Peterborough Railway Society, originally formed to preserve locomotives, had already launched the idea of a heritage railway, at a public meeting in Peterborough Town Hall in March 1971. In 1974 the Peterborough Development Corporation bought a section of the line between Longville junction and Yarwell junction and leased it to the Peterborough Railway Society to operate the railway. On 1 June 1977 the Nene Valley Railway began passenger-carrying operations between Wansford and Orton Mere. In 1986 the line was extended eastwards to a new terminus at Peterborough Nene Valley.

At Wansford station a brand new building, opened in 1995, is used

A 19th-century picture of the original Barnwell station building, above, which has long since disappeared, and the station house, below, which is still there. (Northamptonshire County Council)

Barnwell station house today. (Rodger Smith)

Up to the First World War, Barnwell had a curious custom of 'Singing to the Trains'. On May Day, the village girls dressed in all their finery to accompany the May Garland, which was paraded through the village, ending up on the station platform, where the girls sang every time a train passed through. When a troop of Boy Scots was formed in the village, they were allowed to join the annual procession. This picture is of the 1913 event. (Northamptonshire County Council)

as the headquarters of the NVR. Nearby is the original main station building, which, though Grade II listed, is disused and in need of repair. The NVR is hoping to raise the £160,000 required to buy it. A new down platform has been built and, as already mentioned, a station building from Barnwell has been moved to this site.

Castor station, which was damaged by a 'doodlebug' (a V2 rocket) in the Second World War (the crater can still be seen nearby), has been demolished, although a bit of station forecourt survives as hard standing.

Overton was renamed Orton Waterville on 1 August 1913. In the 19th century, the names Orton and Overton had been used

Oundle station in 1967. Timetabled passenger services had ceased three years before, but the station was still used for occasional special trains for Oundle School. (H.C. Casserley)

almost interchangeably for the two parishes of Orton Waterville and Orton Longueville, but gradually Orton came to prevail. It lost its passenger service in 1942 but was used by railwaymen till 1962. It remained open for freight till December 1964. With the opening of the NVR in 1977 a new station called Ferry Meadows was opened nearby to serve Nene Country Park. The building used for this is the old GNR goods office from Fletton Yard on the East Coast Main Line, saved and moved to this site.

The Nene Valley Railway has been a huge success story, a beacon to heritage railway enthusiasts everywhere. On a summer morning, the telephones in the main office never stop ringing. The emphasis that the NVR has always placed on its educational value has undoubtedly contributed to its success. Thousands of schoolchildren, mainly in organised parties, visit the railway every year.

The NVR is an important centre for the study of the rail

The plaque outside the residence that once was Oundle station. (Rodger Smith)

transport of mail. It has a collection of Royal Mail travelling post-office (TPO) coaches, and can demonstrate the lineside collecting systems (the last recorded mail drop into collecting equipment was at Penrith in October 1971). At one time all long-distance mail went by rail, and the TPOs were essential for prompt delivery.

Nevertheless the volunteer staff are cautious about the future. Administrator Murray Brown explained to me that the big problem is the sheer cost of keeping such a railway going, with its high fixed costs. In the 1960s, when steam was being replaced on BR, many wealthy individuals liked the idea of owning and preserving a steam locomotive. But such owners are now getting

The original Wansford station building, which the Nene Valley Railway are hoping to buy. (Judy Wheldon)

David Ray, education officer for the Nene Valley Railway, has just ushered several parties of schoolchildren aboard a train departing for Yarwell Junction. (Judy Wheldon)

The best-known locomotive on the Nene Valley Railway, and one that would be instantly recognised by children the world over, from Japan to the USA. For the Nene Valley Railway is the permanent home of Thomas the Tank Engine. Thomas is actually Hudswell Clarke 0-6-0T no 1800, built in 1947, and here it is exiting the 617-yard Wansford Tunnel and nearing Yarwell Junction station, the western extremity of the NVR, on 8 April 2007. Yarwell was formerly the junction for the lines to Northampton and Rugby, which closed in 1964 and 1966 respectively. (Murray Brown)

on in years, and many are finding the expenses of keeping their locomotives becoming exorbitant. A complete refurbishment to bring a steam locomotive up to operating condition can run into six-figure sums. However, steam is not the only attraction of a heritage railway; diesel gala days here are more successful with every passing year. The NVR is now regarded as one of the top tourist attractions of the region, with some 60,000 visitors a year. It also gains income from film contracts (it featured, for example, in two James Bond films *Goldeneye* and *Octopussy*) and television programmes, and also from its training facilities.

7

The Stratford-upon-Avon & Midland Junction Railway

The 12.45 pm train to Stratford-upon-Avon waiting to depart at the S&MJR station at Blisworth in April 1952. (H.C. Casserley)

Towcester is the oldest town in Northamptonshire, with a transport history going back nearly 2,000 years. It sits astride the Roman Watling Street, which once echoed to the footsteps of marching legionaries, and today forms the route of the A5 trunk road, busy with a constant stream of cars and lorries.

Somewhere in between the legionaries and the cars came the stagecoaches. Towcester, as the inns along its main street show, was an important coaching centre. So much so that by the early 1800s it had become one of the busiest transport hubs in the country. And so, when the new-fangled railways brought, with startling abruptness, the stagecoach era to an end, Towcester was particularly badly hit. The main London to Birmingham line was

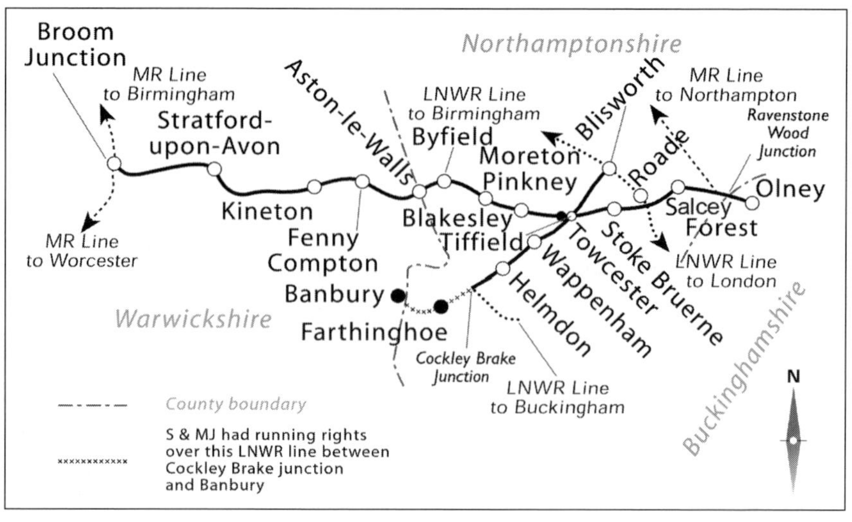

not far away, between 4 and 5 miles, but that was a world away as far as through traffic was concerned. So Towcester went into a deep slumber, lasting 30 years, until finally a railway connection was built from the town to that main line at Blisworth.

This line, so long-awaited, was built by the Northampton & Banbury Junction Railway (N&BJR), one of the forerunners of the Stratford-upon-Avon & Midland Junction Railway (S&MJR). The LNWR already had its station at Blisworth on its London to Birmingham line, and the N&BJR's Blisworth station was built alongside, with a subway linking one to the other. The Blisworth–Towcester line opened in May 1866, and – as so often in Northamptonshire – there were a number of ironstone sidings on this section.

An experiment was made with a passenger station at Tiffield, a simple construction with one timber platform, built on the highest point of the line (Tiffield Summit). However, this station only saw regular services for two years, 1869–1871, although it may have been used for special occasions such as Towcester

A Virgin train thunders along the West Coast Main Line, passing the former junction with the S&JMR at Blisworth. The alignment of the S&MJR is shown by the fence in the right foreground of the picture. (Rodger Smith)

races up to about 1908. It would not have been a popular stop for the locomotive crew, as up trains had a great deal of difficulty in making a standing start on an uphill gradient. This section used to teem with rabbits, and at least one locomotive driver was said to have taken a shotgun along with him to take pot shots. Today a 'pocket park' has been created from the cutting at Tiffield.

In August 1871 the line was extended from Towcester to Helmdon, with an intermediate station at Wappenham. This was only a small village, and the station was closed for passenger traffic in July 1951. Today, at Wappenham, a water treatment works has been built on the line of the railway. Both Wappenham and Helmdon stations were single-platform but with passing loops. Later the line was extended further, to Cockley Brake junction, where it met the LNWR's Bletchley to Banbury line (Chapter 4), and a Blisworth to Banbury service was started. Cockley Brake junction, close by the wood of that name, was given a passing loop, which was used by trains from Verney Junction (via Bletchley) to Towcester, and allowed the engine to run round.

Later, after the Great Central line (Chapter 1) had been built with its own Helmdon (for Sulgrave) station, Helmdon station on the S&MJR became known as Helmdon Village. Paradoxically, the building of the GCR line meant a temporary increase in traffic for the S&MJR, bringing men and materials to the site. It was later given a second platform, but this was only used on race days when trains would pass here. Like Wappenham, Helmdon Village station was closed to passenger traffic in July 1951.

The early history of the S&MJR and associated companies is a long and tortuous one, with plans made and abandoned, insolvencies (on one occasion bailiffs seized a locomotive) and changes of name, too confusing to relate here. Suffice it to say that in 1909, as a result of mergers of several small companies, the S&MJR came into existence. Irreverent wits called it the 'Slow, Miserable and Jolty' line, but then practically every set of railway initials brought forth similar ribald coinings.

While the Towcester to Helmdon line was being created, another of the companies which was to become part of the S&MJR, the East & West Junction Railway, was building a line from a junction with the N&BJR line at Greens Norton (just north of Towcester) to Stratford-upon-Avon in Warwickshire. An elaborate ceremony was held on 3 August 1864, for the cutting of the first sod. This was done by Lady Palmerston, in the presence of her husband Viscount Palmerston, Prime Minister, an indication of how important the line was expected to be. When the line reached Fenny Compton, a junction was made with the GWR Oxford to Birmingham line. A short 6-mile section between

Fenny Compton and Kineton opened in 1871, but the remaining sections were not ready until 1873.

Towcester station, in expectation of becoming an important rail centre, had been given one up and two down platforms at the station, and extensive sidings. However, passenger numbers proved so disappointing, and company finances became so perilous, that between 1877 and 1885 all stopping passenger services were suspended.

After the coming into being of the merged S&MJR, the line between Blisworth and Stratford-upon-Avon promoted itself for a time in the early 20th century as the 'Shakespeare Route'. This catchphrase was used in all its communications. It was an opportune moment, for American tourists had now started to come to visit Stratford in some numbers, and the railways were still almost the only way of getting there. The LNWR, which had running rights on the E&WJR, took advantage of this to run direct trains from Euston to Stratford. The S&JMR also gained running rights over LNWR lines from Blisworth to Northampton, and from Cockley Brake junction to Banbury.

It was all very promising. A major Shakespeare festival was scheduled to take place in Stratford in 1910, and was expected to provide a major boost for the line. But the death of King Edward VII led to the festival being cancelled. This proved to be an unfortunate setback for the line's tourist potential, from which it had not recovered when the First World War broke out.

In the 1923 Grouping the S&MJR, with 47 miles and 46 chains of track, became part of the LMS. In 1932 experiments were tried with a Ro Railer, a rail-bus that ran on rails from Blisworth to Stratford, and then ran on roads to the Welcombe Hotel, built by the LMS specifically for tourist traffic. This was a unique vehicle, and a set of levers raised and lowered the rail and road wheels as appropriate. All four road wheels could be raised within five

In 1957 locomotive no 44076 heads into Towcester station from Northampton with a goods pick-up train. The footbridge on the left of the picture connected platforms 2 & 3 (the goods train is passing platform 3) with the main station buildings. (Ken Fairey)

minutes. This was an attempt to solve the problem of compatible road and rail transport, which had vexed designers ever since the 18th century break-through in vehicle adhesion, when the flange necessary to keep a rail vehicle on track had been moved from the rail to the wheel.

The Ro Railer could take 26 seated passengers. Typical timetabling was for a departure from the Welcombe Hotel at 4.10 pm, arrive Stratford-upon-Avon LMS station at 4.20 and depart at 4.30, call at Towcester, then arrive at Blisworth at 5.32 in plenty of time for the Euston train on the West Coast Main Line at 7.10 pm. The vehicle then departed Blisworth in the opposite direction at 6 pm, again called at Towcester, arrived at Stratford station at 7.10, left again at 7.15, and arrived at the Welcombe Hotel at 7.25 pm.

The experiment excited a lot of curiosity, and if it had been a success the history of modern transport would have been very different. However, there were several breakdowns, and it quickly became apparent that such a vehicle had difficulty with gradients. It also failed commercially, nowhere near achieving the expected take-up in visitors, and the hybrid vehicle ceased to run after 2 July 1932, after only three months in service. It was replaced by a 0-4-4 tank engine pulling a single coach.

Another tourist attraction for the line was Towcester Racecourse, known especially for the Grafton Hunt steeplechase on Easter Monday, which could bring between 7,000 and 8,000 passengers to the town. Between 1927 and 1939 there was a regular excursion service to Towcester races directly from London St Pancras.

In the 1920s, around 9 am on a weekday, Towcester station was at its busiest, with three passenger trains about to depart, one for Banbury, one for Broom and one for Blisworth.

Stations on the 'Shakespeare Route' within Northamptonshire, between Towcester and Fenny Compton, were Blakesley, Moreton Pinkney (called Morton Pinkney on some station signs), Byfield and Aston-le-Walls.

Blakesley was the most curious station on the line, because it connected with a narrow (15 inch) gauge railway that ran to Blakesley Hall. This little railway, with its own platform at Blakesley station, was built in 1903 by Charles William Bartholomew, the local squire and owner of the hall. He was a civil engineer and began by laying out a railway in his own grounds. He then got permission to run the ¼-mile section down to Blakesley station. The line carried coal, farm supplies and occasional visitors. It began with two Cagney locomotives and modified carriages and trucks, but eventually used a petrol-driven locomotive *Balcovesley* (designed to look like a steam engine) built by the Northampton firm of Bassett-Lowke. C.W. Bartholomew died in 1919, but his widow allowed the line to remain and trains to run on special occasions. In 1939 the system was sold off to an estate in Yorkshire, and the track was lifted in 1940. Blakesley Hall was used as a hospital in the Second World War, but after other miscellaneous uses, becoming steadily more dilapidated, it was demolished in 1957.

Byfield station – the only place between Towcester and Stratford where engines could take on water – has also disappeared.

Aston-le-Walls was going to be bypassed, but after petitioning from local farmers and landowners, the S&MJR put in a public siding in 1910, which had its own short platform and was situated 2 miles 10 chains from Byfield station. It was closed in 1953.

Yet another company (it had the impossibly long name of Easton Neston Mineral & Towcester, Roade & Olney Junction Railway) which was to become part of the S&MJR embarked on a scheme to build a line east from Towcester to a connection

Blakesley station in 1958. (H.C. Casserley)

H.C. Casserley's 1958 picture of Blakesley was taken from the top of the bridge in this picture. Looking through the bridge today from what was track level we can see that a modern bungalow has been built right across the trackbed. (Rodger Smith)

with the Midland Railway's Northampton to Bedford line at Ravenstone Wood junction. This line opened in 1891. There was a short spur to the LNWR's Roade station, and stations at Stoke Bruerne and Salcey Forest. Stoke Bruerne station was nearly a mile from the village, on the Blisworth road.

Salcey Forest station was in an isolated spot, accessed only by a bridle road (today part of the Midshires Way long-distance footpath), and the reason for building it and the substantial station buildings (finally demolished some 50 years ago) was something of a mystery. One theory is that it was put there at the behest of the Fitzroy family who lived at a large house nearby, Salcey Lawn. It was used by troop trains during the Second World War.

This railway was known at one time as the 'Bread and Scrape Line', presumably as a reference to its shaky financial position. Passenger services began on 1 December 1892, but a local paper reported that only one passenger got off and one got on at Salcey Forest on the first service train. Stopping services for Stoke Bruerne and Salcey Forest were withdrawn on 23 March 1893 and never restored, though sometimes special trains and excursions called at the two stations. The substantial station buildings at Stoke Bruerne station were turned into a private house, and, astonishingly, the platform is still there. By the time the 1905 Ordnance Survey map was produced it was shown only as a 'mineral line'.

However, the London St Pancras to Towcester race day excursions, mentioned above, used this section of the line. When this particular service began in 1927 it was the first passenger train to use the Ravenstone Wood junction to Towcester section since 30 March 1893. In 1930 a race special for Central Board staff ran from Newmarket to Stratford. There were also instances of enthusiasts' specials stopping at Stoke Bruerne and Salcey.

The S&MJR became part of the LMS at Grouping in 1923. The LMS started to run excursion trains from 1937 from London to Stratford over what had become the freight-only Towcester–Olney line, stopping at Bedford and Towcester. Stratford and Towcester were the only towns on the line and both had comparatively small populations (8,500 and 2,775 respectively).

In the inter-war period special goods trains carrying bananas, the Banana Specials, ran from Avonmouth docks (near Bristol) to Somers Town (the goods depot for St Pancras) using the S&JMR route.

On nationalisation in 1948 the section from Fenny Compton to Blisworth and on to Ravenstone Wood junction became part of the London Midland region, while the Warwickshire section of the line, between Fenny Compton and Broom Junction, went

S&MJR trackbed near what was once the site of Salcey Forest station. (Rodger Smith)

to the Western region (which closed the Stratford to Broom section on 13 June 1960). The Banbury to Towcester section closed on 30 June 1951 and the Blisworth to Stratford section on 7 April 1952. The line between Towcester and Cockley Brake junction was lifted towards the end of 1955. Blisworth S&MJR station closed on 1 January 1960. The last known passenger train on the S&MJR was a special charter by the Stephenson Locomotive Society, which ran on 24 April 1965 from Birmingham Snow Hill to Woodford Halse.

The line between Towcester and Ravenstone Wood junction was still heavily used by freight, running between Wales and north-east England, until it was closed in June 1958. The Towcester–Olney line had to be closed because of the building of

Enthusiasts take pictures of locomotive 43222 hauling a rail tour special as it halts at Byfield station in April 1956. The water tower can be clearly seen in the foreground, as can the station's goods siding. (H.C. Casserley)

Towcester station buildings and station forecourt in 1965, after closure. (H.C. Casserley)

Detail from the 13-ft model of Towester station, now in the Birmingham Museums Collection. (Rodger Smith)

Moreton Pinkney station is now an industrial site, with access strictly forbidden except for commercial visitors. The old station buildings have been completely removed. However, as the picture shows, the site still carries the station name. (Rodger Smith)

the M1 motorway. During the very weekend of actual closure the embankment at Quinton Green, east of Roade, was breached.

Helmdon and Wappenham closed in July 1951, Towcester, Blakesley, Moreton Pinkney in April 1952 and Byfield in November 1952. The section from Woodford West junction to Blisworth closed even to goods on 3 February 1964. The whole former S&MJR network had completely closed by the end of the 1950s. Towcester station was one of those that was totally demolished. Helmdon station buildings were used as a bus garage.

8
The Harringworth
Viaduct Line

The Harringworth Viaduct, seen from Seaton in Rutland (the building in the foreground is the former Seaton station). (Rodger Smith)

By the 1870s the Midland Railway was considering how best to create an additional north–south route which would also exploit Northamptonshire's iron ore production.

It already had its main line from Derby through Leicester, Market Harborough and Kettering, which was proving so successful it was beginning to worry about congestion. The solution it came up with was to run a branch from its existing west-to-east Syston junction to Peterborough line. The point at which the branch started became Manton Junction. The branch ran south to a point 2 miles north of Kettering station, where it joined the Midland main line.

The route was surveyed in the spring and early summer

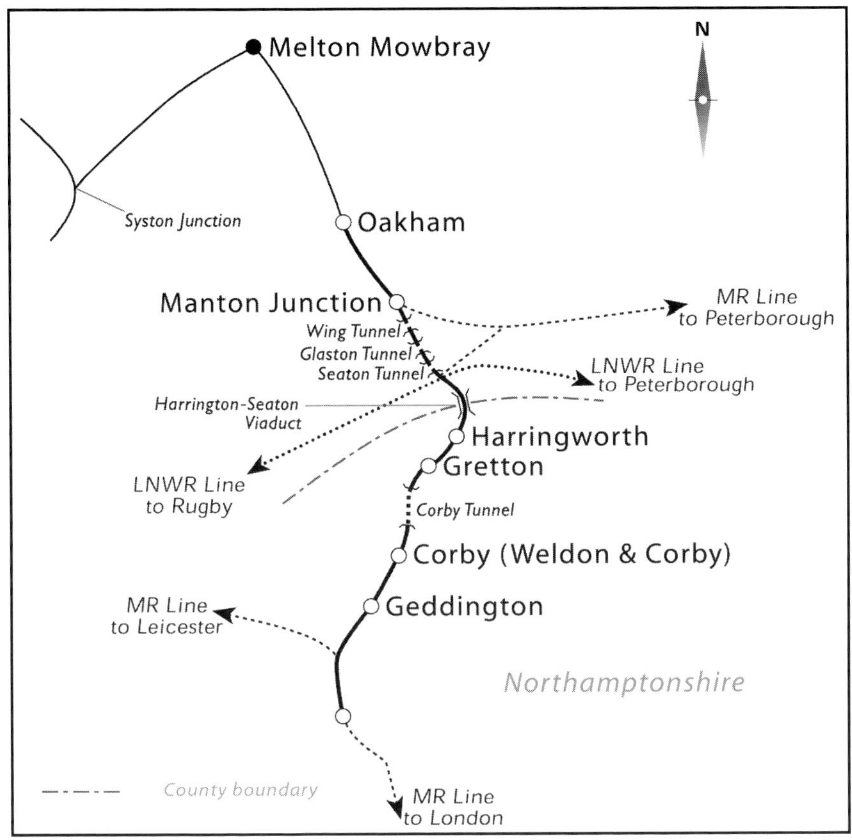

of 1875. In June the contractors cut the first ceremonial sod at Rushton crossroads. But this was a difficult line to build. The valleys in Northamptonshire, particularly those of its two principal rivers, the Welland and the Nene, run west to east, and so the new line had to go across the grain of the landscape. In its 15¾ miles it needed four tunnels (Seaton, Glaston, Corby and Wing), the second and third of which were more than a mile long, 16 cuttings, 12 embankments, three short viaducts and the stupendously long and high Harringworth Viaduct.

One particular problem was with Glendon cutting, with its

thick vein of ironstone. A total of 260,000 cubic yards of earth was extracted from the cutting, and of these some 100,000, it was calculated, were ironstone. Rushton cutting had to be made through blue lias clay, which is very tenacious and difficult to dig out. Corby cutting, one mile 14 chains in length and 56 ft in depth, required the excavation of 500,000 cubic yards of earth. More than half this excavated material was taken to the tunnel to create an embankment 2 miles to the north.

Glaston Tunnel, nearly as long as Corby Tunnel, had to be bored through heavy ground which built up high crushing pressures, and the bore required huge amounts of timbering support. But the greatest challenge of all was the crossing of the wide Welland valley. This required the construction of the Harringworth Viaduct (also known as the Welland Viaduct), the longest non-urban railway viaduct in the British Isles. It is 1,275 yards long, with 82 arches each of 40 ft in width and with an average height of 57 ft. It is estimated that over 10 million bricks were used in the viaduct's construction. One calculation is that if the bricks were used to form a pathway 63 inches wide it would stretch from London to York. The bricks were made from local clay at nearby Seaton Yard, but Derbyshire gritstone was brought in for constructing the springers, string courses and copings. A banquet was held on 17 July 1878 to celebrate the keying of the last of the 82 arches. The celebration took place in a large shed near Seaton station.

The construction of the line kept 2,500 men employed for more than one year, and at its peak the workforce reached 3,500. The various trades included miners, navvies, labourers, carpenters, blacksmiths, bricklayers and brickmakers. Some workers were local people, and others found lodgings in villages along the line. But around 1,500 men, some of whom had their families with them (307 women and 700 children), were accommodated in 205 huts, 26 at Rushton, 50 at Corby, 12 at Gretton, 70 at Glaston and 47 at Seaton.

Harringworth station in the 1930s, looking north. The train in the picture has just come off the viaduct. (Stations UK)

The work on the whole line was completed by December 1879, when goods traffic started. A local passenger service started in March 1880, then on 1 June 1880 a long distance service from Leeds to London via Sheffield, Nottingham and Kettering. Stations were opened at Harringworth, Gretton, Corby and Geddington.

On 1 October 1916 a Zeppelin dropped incendiary bombs on the line, near the entrance to the 1,920-yard Corby Tunnel, but there was no damage.

When the line was built Corby was just another Northamptonshire village, and the station was called Corby & Cottingham (later Weldon & Corby, then Corby & Weldon, and then just Corby). But in the excavations for Corby Tunnel iron ore deposits were revealed, and as Corby was close to other sources of good quality iron ore, it grew into a steel-making town. In the mid-1930s it became the site of one of the country's largest steel-making plants. Workers were badly needed, and many of them were recruited from Scotland, especially after giant steelmaker Stewart & Lloyd decided to concentrate production at Corby and shut its Scottish plant. Even today, Corby retains much of its Scottish influence – it is, for example, the only town in England to have supporters' clubs for both Glasgow Rangers and Glasgow Celtic.

The production of steel brought a great deal of freight traffic to the line, particularly in the inter-war years. During the war years the steel furnaces were working flat out to maintain production, and this high production rate continued for some years after the war, before it began to level off and then decline. Steel production finally ended at Corby – which not so long before had been England's leading steel-making town – in the 1980s.

The inter-war period also marked an increase in a particular type of passenger traffic, from seaside holidays and seaside excursion day-trips, and village stations along the line benefited from these.

In the days when the Midland Railway employed dray horses for local deliveries, those horses were brought to Geddington for an annual 'holiday' of lush grazing and no work. Geddington, usually one of the quieter stations, had its busiest day on 20 June 1945. The Second World War had just ended, and one of the major US Air Force bombing fleets, the 401st Bombardment Group, had been based at Deenethorpe, east of Corby. They were one of the first groups to be returned to the United States, and while the air crew flew their planes home, all the ground staff embarked on that day at Geddington station in a series of trains, which took them up to Gurrock in Scotland to board the *Queen Elizabeth*.

The first stations on the line to close were Harringworth and Geddington, in November 1948. When the line was re-signalled and the signal box from Harringworth became redundant, it was acquired by the Nene Valley Railway and moved to Wansford. In

Gretton station in 1959 showing (above) platforms and (below) station frontage. (H.C. Casserley)

Gretton station building today, now a private residence. The gate on the left of the picture is an access to the track still owned by the railway authorities. (Rodger Smith)

April 1966 Gretton station was closed and turned into a private residence.

At the same time Corby station was closed. This seemed an amazing decision, and even more so when the line between Corby and Kettering was singled. A bus connection was provided, until, between 1987 and 1990, an hourly rail shuttle service between Corby and Kettering was reinstated. But after 1990 it was back to the bus service. There are constant calls for a rail service to be reinstated for Corby, which in 2007 had the unenviable distinction of being the largest town in England (some claim the largest town in Europe) without a railway station, and there are encouraging signs that a new station, and a new rail service, will be provided. There is a £1.2 million pound scheme for a new station, with a

A railbus service pictured outside Kettering station in 1976. (Rodger Smith)

Site of the old Corby station. (Author)

taxi rank and a car park for 140 cars. Meanwhile a bus depot has been built near the site of the old station, the buildings and structures of which have been completely removed.

Today the line is still open for goods traffic, but apart from the Corby–Kettering section there is no suggestion of a regular passenger service ever being reinstated. However, in emergencies, passenger trains may be diverted over this route. Your author and his wife, returning home from London one evening in February 2008, had their train diverted over this because of repair works on the Midland main line. So with Corby being re-opened, and the recurring need for diversions, the Harringworth Viaduct line may soon cease to be a lost line for passenger services.

The Midland Railway: Kettering to Huntingdon

A Cambridge-bound train entering Thrapston Midland Road station in 1955. (Stations UK)

Once again the richness of iron ore deposits in Northamptonshire led to the building of a railway line. This one was built by a company called the Kettering, Thrapston & Huntingdon Railway, although from the outset they were closely linked with the Midland Railway, and it was arranged that the MR would work the line (at 40% of the total income for the first seven years, and then 50%). The KT&HR became completely absorbed by the MR in 1897.

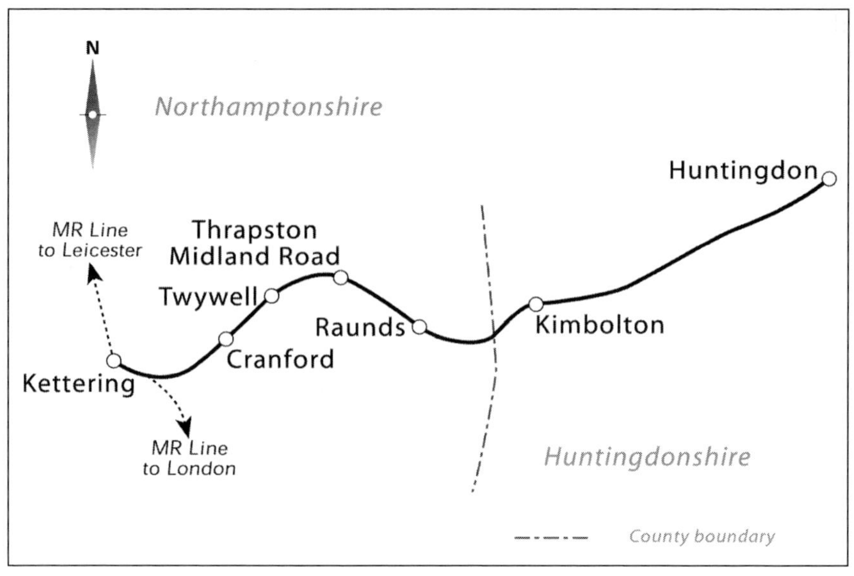

This railway opened in 1866, primarily as a freight line, with substantial iron ore traffic. There was some provision for passengers, though they were not a priority. And because it was a largely rural route, there were comparatively few passenger trains. Nevertheless stations were built at Cranford, Twywell, Thrapston (called Thrapston Midland Road to distinguish it from the LNWR station on the Northampton to Peterborough line) and Raunds in Northamptonshire, and Kimbolton, Long Stow, Grafham, Buckden and Huntingdon in Huntingdonshire. Running powers were obtained from the Great Eastern Railway to continue via St Ives (Huntingdonshire) to Cambridge, which meant that – for passenger promotion purposes – the line eventually became known as the 'Varsity line'. Much of the line was single-track with passing loops.

The line was said to be one of the prettiest in the Midland counties, running through orchards and water meadows. After the Second World War there were three trains a day in each direction, but no Sunday service. Special excursions to East Coast resorts such as Great Yarmouth and Hunstanton ran in the summer months.

Exhaustion of ironstone deposits, such as those at Cranford and Thrapston, threatened the survival of the line, since it was obviously not viable as a mainly passenger route, but as with so many railways there was a stay of execution when the Second World War brought extra traffic – commercial road traffic had practically ceased and there was increased demand for transport of armaments and service personnel. However, this respite was only temporary. After the war the low takings from passenger traffic were obvious. The first station to close, in 1951, was Twywell, and then Cranford closed to passengers in April 1956. Thrapston and Raunds closed in June 1959, but stayed as goods stations until the closing months of 1963. After this the line was used almost solely for goods trains carrying processed iron from the Twywell area, and when these ceased in 1978 the line was closed altogether, and the track was lifted.

Today the first part of the line, where it branched off the Midland main line at Kettering junction, can easily be traced, because a footpath from Polwell Lane in the Kettering suburb of Barton Seagrave, immediately north of the A14, uses part of the old trackbed, including a high embankment and a bridge over the River Ise. The footpath can be followed back almost all the way to the junction. East of Kettering, however, there is little to be seen of the old railway, for the route has disappeared under the modern A14, a busy dual carriageway which carries traffic from the M1 to Felixstowe and other ports.

The villagers at Cranford St John had the rare privilege of having a railway station in the middle of the village, rare because in the 19th century the locations of stations were determined to suit railway builders rather than railway users. Cranford station, a handsome stone structure, has been converted into a private house.

A quiet moment at Cranford station in the 1930s, on this single-track line. (Stations UK)

Plaque at the former Cranford station, now a private residence. (Rodger Smith)

Twywell station house, now a private residence. (Rodger Smith)

Twywell station, more typically, was inconveniently remote from the village. To see for yourself just how inconvenient, it is necessary to take the road east out of the village, and then a footpath to a footbridge over the A14, then follow the path which takes another footbridge over a stream and crosses a field. This brings you to the old Kettering road, now cut off by the A14, and from this you can look down to the old Twywell station house, now, like so many others, converted into a private residence.

East of Twywell were the important Islip iron-working furnaces, once a major industrial complex with its own narrow gauge rail system. All has now completely disappeared. An industrial estate occupies part of the site today.

At Thrapston, however, the most important remaining architectural feature of the line is still intact. This is the 15-arch

In May 1965 locomotive 45660 hauling an iron ore train is about to pass the former Twywell station, where other iron ore trucks stand waiting. (Ken Fairey)

An early view of Raunds station. The cattle pens and goods sheds can be seen in the rear of the picture. (Lens of Sutton)

Raunds station site today. (Rodger Smith)

H.C. Casserley took this picture of Raunds station in April 1959, with locomotive no 46403 entering the station with the 4.55 pm Cambridge to Kettering train.

viaduct over the River Nene, which replaced an earlier wooden structure. Thrapston also had its ironstone workings, with its narrow gauge railway connecting to the goods yard of the station. The buildings of Thrapston Midland Road station, which was located on the southern edge of the town but not too far from its centre, still exist but are in a dilapidated state following a fire.

After Thrapston the line, which had been following an easterly direction, turned south. The station for Raunds, also a small town, was highly inconvenient for the residents, being 2 miles from the populated area. This location seems to have been almost perverse, since the whole area is level with hardly any contour variation. The explanation seems to lie in the concentration on freight, and the need for space to manoeuvre it. As well as minerals Raunds station also handled cattle, and the station yard included cattle pens.

10
The Midland Railway: Northampton to Bedford

Piddington station in 1955, facing Northampton, taken from a passing train. It certainly looks – from the prominent greenhouse and garden shed – as if the stationmaster was a keen gardener. (H.C. Casserley)

Moving to the south-east of the county, we find a line that linked the county towns of Northampton and Bedford, built by the Midland Railway and opened in 1872.

As a grand gesture to the citizens of Northampton the Midland Railway built an imposing and centrally situated new station, Northampton St John's, built in the grounds of the former St John's Priory. Opened in 1872, it was a massive building, too ambitious for the amount of traffic through it, like some other

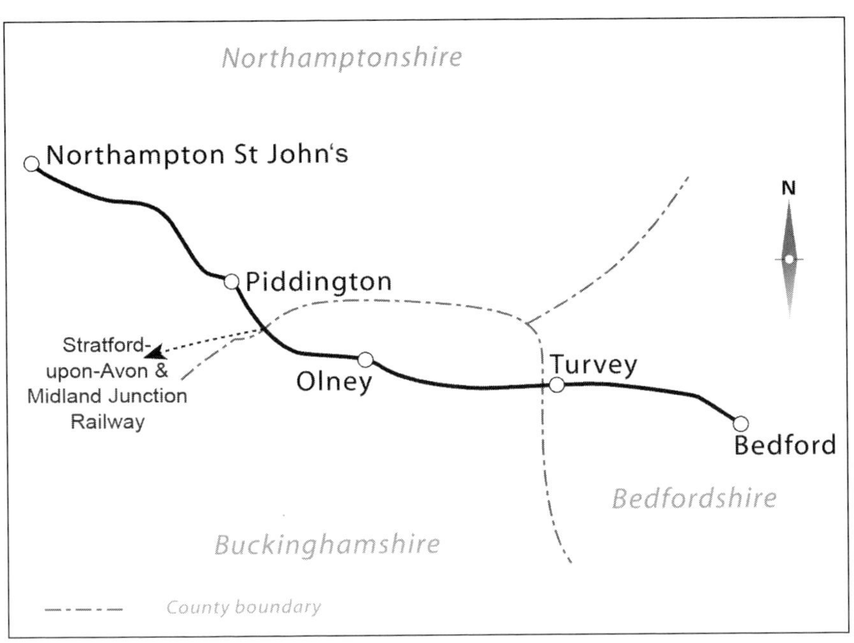

A sign in Northampton today – the sole reminder that the large elegant St John's station once stood here. (Rodger Smith)

Piddington station buildings today, now a private residence. (Rodger Smith)

Next to it is the industrial site still known as Station Farm. (Rodger Smith)

A two-coach Huntingdon-bound train calls at Piddington station on 15 March 1962, only two weeks before the station closed. (Ken Fairey)

stations along the line. The trains left St John's southwards on imposing arches above the road.

This station, which had become an LMS station at Grouping, was closed on 3 July 1939, and from then the services ran into Northampton Castle. St John's station buildings were demolished in 1960 to make way for a car park.

Intermediate stations between Northampton and Bedford (Piddington in Northamptonshire, Olney in Buckinghamshire and Turvey in Bedfordshire) were closed on 5 March 1962.

Piddington, a small station in the middle of nowhere, was a long way from the village from which it took its name, and in fact was nearer to two other villages, Horton and Hackleton (the station was called Piddington & Horton from 1876–1904). It was given buildings on the same scale as Olney, a much larger place. Piddington station was noted for its spick and span appearance, and for its flowerbeds. As there was a large Ministry of Defence store in Piddington, with its own branch, the line between Northampton and Piddington remained open, administered by the Ministry from 1968, until the 1980s. Most of the track on this section had been lifted by 1986. All that remains is a comparatively short stretch south of Northampton to the Brackmills Industrial Estate.

11
The Midland Railway: Wellingborough to Higham Ferrers

The 4.15 pm to Wellingborough leaving Higham Ferrers on an August day in 1945. (H.C. Casserley)

This was the last passenger branch line to be built in Northamptonshire, and was prompted by the rapid growth, in the second half of the 19th century, of the boot and shoe making centre of Rushden.

The branch, from Wellingborough, was created in 1892–1893 by the Midland Railway. Though the trackbed was made wide enough for eventual doubling, it remained single-line throughout

This picture of Higham Ferrers station before demolition shows what a handsome structure it was. (Lens of Sutton)

its existence. The line was continued beyond Rushden to Higham Ferrers. The intention was to extend the line to Raunds, to create a through route and join up with the 'Varsity line' (described in Chapter 9), but it proved impossible to overcome the opposition of a key landowner.

Rushden was always the most important place served by this branch, and before the First World War the station there had a staff of 32, including clerks, carters and porters. In the 1930s Rushden shoe manufacturers would charter special trains to take their employees and families on seaside excursions. Regular passenger services ceased in 1959, though holiday specials to Blackpool and Great Yarmouth continued to use the line until 1964. An enthusiasts' special ran up the line on 18 May 1968. Goods services continued, with gravel from local

A 1940s-themed day at today's Rushden station. (Rodger Smith)

Interior of the stationmaster's office at Rushden, with a coal fire burning, and papers ready to hand, just as if he had left it for a few minutes, instead of 40 years ago. (Author)

workings making up an important part of the traffic, together with coal for the Rushden gasworks. The closure of the Rushden gasworks after the conversion of homes from coal-derived gas to North Sea Gas, which happened in 1968, was a blow to the economics of the line. The gravel trains continued to run right up to 3 November 1969, when the line was closed to all traffic. The station buildings at Rushden, including the goods shed, were bought by Northamptonshire County Council, and were used for some years as a warehouse. In 1984 it was leased to a local enthusiasts' group, the Rushden Historical Transport Society. This society eventually acquired the freehold in 1996. In 1999 the society gained the lease of a quarter of a mile of the trackbed, and rails were laid. The society's operating arm, known as the Rushden, Higham, & Wellingborough Railway, runs demonstration trains at weekends. It also has ambitious long-term plans to extend further towards Higham Ferrers and, ultimately, to restore the line back to Wellingborough. As we saw in Chapter 6 there had been a station called Higham Ferrers on the Northampton to Peterborough line, even though it was nearer to Irthlingborough than Higham Ferrers, and was eventually to be renamed as Irthlingborough. When that station opened a horse-drawn coach operated a service from it to the town square and the Wheatsheaf Inn at Rushden.

A walnut tree stood on railway property near Higham Ferrers station, and was widely famed for its produce. At one time some 20 lb of walnuts were being sent every year to the St Pancras Hotel. The station itself, a handsome structure in stone, has been demolished. It is not known what happened to the walnut tree.

Conclusion

The best way of remembering lost railways is to revive them as heritage lines. As we have seen, there are three of these in Northamptonshire – the Nene Valley Railway (one of the biggest in the country), the Northampton & Lamport Railway and the Rushden, Higham & Wellingborough Railway.

But are they over-dependent on nostalgia for the great days of steam locomotion? And, if that is the case, is there a generation problem? As the last generation that remembers steam enters old age, and begins to die off, will there be enough volunteers, for example, to keep the country's many heritage railways in existence? There is also the problem of the high cost of maintenance of steam locomotives. These locomotives were often saved from the scrapheap in the 1960s by wealthy enthusiasts, who themselves are no longer young. How long will they be able or even prepared to pay out £300,000 or more for the refurbishment of their cherished engine?

These are problems that all heritage railways have to face. Fortunately all three Northamptonshire revival lines seem to be run with efficiency and panache, and all three were well patronised on the days when we visited. The Nene Valley Railway is certainly right to emphasise educational aspects. Railways are interwoven with the industrial and commercial life of Britain, and their operating systems were a triumph of engineering and organisation. Heritage railways are working museums, with all the sights and sounds, and even smells, of living history.

Another use for old railway trackbeds is for footpaths and cycleways. Northamptonshire is less well known than many other counties – Devon, or Derbyshire, to give two examples – for outdoor activities in the countryside, but it does have tourist attractions that deserve to be better celebrated. The honey-coloured stone of which so many Northamptonshire houses are constructed gives it some of the prettiest villages in the country. As the lost railways of Northamptonshire are largely rural routes, serving many such villages, and as many of the trackbeds can still be traced on the ground, there is surely potential for their development for tourism.

We met Steven Hollowell, Definitive Map team leader for the Northamptonshire County Council, who agreed about their potential, particularly in the west of the county, though the financial stringency under which all local authorities now have to operate would prevent any large-scale development in the immediate future. He mentioned, however, the national Lost Ways Project, under which funding was available for opening up paths as rights of way if continuous use for 20 years or more could be shown. The Brampton Valley Way, mentioned in Chapter 5, is a pointer as to what can be done. As we saw in Chapter 3 there is a possibility that Sustrans, the national sustainable transport agency, may become involved in developing a Daventry to Braunston path using the route of the Weedon to Leamington line. A further extension, using the trackbed to Wolfhampcote and beyond, could be linked with an attractive canal towpath to provide a circular walk from Braunston. Such developments would undoubtedly enhance the tourist attraction of Braunston, which has already become a major centre for inland waterways pleasure craft.

In the local studies department of Northamptonshire County Library (with its ever-helpful and enthusiastic staff) we came across a report, *Disused Railways of Northamptonshire*, produced by the county council planning office in 1971. This found that there were 129 miles (including 1¼ miles in tunnels) of standard gauge former railway lines in the county, all of which had been surveyed. The dry language of an official report becomes almost poetical when it describes what they came across:

> One noticeable feature of all lines, especially those abandoned some time ago, is the abundance of wildlife, obvious even to the casual observer. During the course of the surveys rabbits, horses, foxes, wild birds and badgers' setts were seen to advantage. Wild flowers not normally seen elsewhere were observed and a number of places have a very tranquil atmosphere.

But converting the trackbeds to recreational use presented many problems to the planners even then. One problem was that of ownership. In many cases – even as early as 1971 – British Rail had sold the land, often to adjacent landowners. Only in nine places were stretches found that might lend themselves to development. Nine schemes were suggested as possibly feasible, and one, turning 35 acres of railway marshalling sidings into woodland at Woodford Halse, is one which has come to pass. Another scheme was for the path along the Daventry–Braunston line, the very route that is now being actively considered by Sustrans.

When lines were opened there were often celebrations, normally in the form of dinners for the directors, investors, and sympathetic local landlords or members of local authorities. Sometimes the celebrations were threefold – for the passage of the enabling Act through Parliament, for cutting the first sod, and for the arrival of the first train. Celebrations for closure usually took the form of sad crowds gathering to watch the last train go by. Let us hope that there will be new celebrations to come, of more and more of the lost railways of Northamptonshire being given a new purpose.

Bibliography

Biddle, Gordon *Britain's Historic Railway Buildings* Oxford University Press, 2003 (ISBN 0 1986 6247 5)

Blagrove, David *The Railways of Northamptonshire* Wharfside Publications, Stoke Bruerne, 2005 (ISBN 1 8719 1820 0)

Blagrove, David *Northamptonshire's Lost Railways* Stenlake Publishing (ISBN 1 8403 3251 4)

Brown, Cynthia *Northampton 1835–1985: Shoe Town, New Town* Phillimore & Co (ISBN 0 8503 3767 4)

Butler, Peter *A History of the Railways of Northamptonshire* Silver Link Publishing Ltd, Great Addington, Northamptonshire (ISBN 1 8579 4281 7)

Dunn, J.M. *The Stratford & Midland Junction Railway* Oakwood Press, 1952

Ellis, Hamilton *The Midland Railway*, Ian Allan Ltd, 1953

Gough, John *The Northampton and Harborough Line* Railway & Canal Historical Society, 1984 (ISBN 0 9014 6135 0)

Hawkins, Mac *The Great Central, Then and Now* BCA 1992

Jordan, Arthur *The Stratford-upon-Avon & Midland Junction Railway – The Shakespeare Route* Oxford Railway Publishing Co, 1982 (ISBN 8 6093 1315)

Mitchell, Vic, Keith Smith, Christopher Awdry and Allan Mott *Branch Lines Around Huntingdon: Kettering to Cambridge* Middleton Press 1991 (ISBN 0 9065 2093 2)

Northamptonshire County Planning Office: *Disused Railways of Northamptonshire* Report 1971

Railway World, November 1982, article: 'The Rushden and Higham Ferrers Branch'

Rice, Alan and Andrew Swift *Northamptonshire Railway Stations on Old Picture Postcards* Reflections of a Bygone Age, Keyworth, Nottinghamshire, 1999 (ISBN 1 9001 3832 8)

Rhodes, John *The Nene Valley Railway* Turntable Publications, Sheffield, 1983 (ISBN 9 0284 4601)

Riley, R.C. and Bill Simpson *A History of the Stratford-upon-Avon and Midland Junction Railway* Lamplight Publications (ISBN 1 8992 4604 5)

Rolt, L.T.C. *The Making of a Railway* Hugh Evelyn Ltd, 1971

Simpson, Bill *Banbury to Verney Junction Branch* Oxford Publishing Co, 1978 (ISBN 9 0288 8870)

Welbourn, Nigel: *Lost lines – LMR* Ian Allan Publishing, 1994 (ISBN 0 711 0277 1)

Williams, Roy *The Midland Railway, a New History* David & Charles, 1988

WEBSITES

Blisworth: www.blisworth.org.uk (a collection of railway pictures)

Nene Valley Railway: www.nvr.org.uk

Northampton & Lamport Railway: www.nlr.org.uk

Rushden, Higham & Wellingborough Railway: www.rhts.co.uk

Index